INSPIRED

INSPIRED
The
Powerful Presence
of the
Holy Spirit

FR. GARY CASTER

servant
AN IMPRINT OF
FRANCISCAN MEDIA
Cincinnati, Ohio

Unless otherwise noted, Scripture texts in this work are taken from the *New American Bible, revised edition* © 2010, 1991, 1986, 1970 Confraternity of Christian Doctrine, Washington, D.C., and are used by permission of the copyright owner. All Rights Reserved. No part of the *New American Bible* may be reproduced in any form without permission in writing from the copyright owner. Scripture passages marked *RSV* have been taken from the *Revised Standard Version*, Catholic edition. Copyright 1946, 1952, 1971 by the Division of Christian Education of the National Council of Churches of Christ in the USA. Used by permission. All rights reserved. Quotes are taken from the English translation of the *Catechism of the Catholic Church* for the United States of America (indicated as *CCC*), 2nd ed. Copyright 1997 by United States Catholic Conference—Libreria Editrice Vaticana.

Cover and book design by Mark Sullivan
Cover image © Fotolia | 2happy

LIBRARY OF CONGRESS CATALOGING-IN-PUBLICATION DATA
Caster, Gary, 1961-
Inspired : the powerful presence of the Holy Spirit / Fr. Gary C. Caster.
pages cm
ISBN 978-1-61636-818-0 (alk. paper)
1. Holy Spirit. 2. Catholic Church—Doctrines. I. Title.
BT121.3.C37 2015
231'.3—dc23
2014037893

ISBN 978-1-61636-818-0

Published by Servant Books, an imprint of Franciscan Media
28 W. Liberty St.
Cincinnati, OH 45202
www.FranciscanMedia.org

Printed in the United States of America.
Printed on acid-free paper.
15 16 17 18 19 5 4 3 2 1

*For the great company of friends
the Holy Spirit has brought into my life.*

CONTENTS

*T*he first time Paul arrives in Ephesus, he finds some disciples living there, "about twelve of them" (Acts 19:7, *RSV*). Encouraged by their presence and being pastorally attentive, Paul asks them, "Did you receive the Holy Spirit?" Their answer is the reason I've chosen to write this book: "We have never even heard that there is a Holy Spirit" (19:2, *RSV*). Being a true evangelist, St. Paul immediately springs into action.

It's my experience that this small group in Ephesus represents the lived situation of many Roman Catholics as well as many other Christians. Although they have surely heard of the Holy Spirit, and perhaps even been confirmed, they aren't entirely clear about the identity and activity of this divine Person. Fixing the mind and heart on Jesus and the Father is naturally easier than fixing them on the member of the Trinity who until fairly recently was referred to as "Ghost." While the humanity of Jesus can bring the mystery of the unseen God nearer to us, language about the Spirit can unintentionally push believers away. How do we relate to that which cannot be seen?

St. Paul's question is but one of many indications from the New Testament Scriptures of the essential role of the Holy Spirit in the life of the early Church. Paul knows that this small group in Ephesus will be able to grow in their relationship with Christ and as a community only through, with, and in the gifts the Holy Spirit imparts. By calling down the Spirit upon them, St. Paul opens up their relationship to Christ in new and unheard-of ways and opens them—viscerally—to the event of Pentecost.

Knowledge and lived experience of the Holy Spirit are no less significant today, because apart from the Holy Spirit there can be no Church. Thus it seems to me that an integral aspect of the New Evangelization should be a catechesis on the Holy Spirit that both encourages and enables a person to be drawn into a more lively relationship with the "Advocate," who has been sent to guide us to all truth and who always pleads our cause. Since it is the Spirit who unites us with Christ, how can we bring Christ to the world if we do not know the Holy Spirit?

For over forty years now, much of this vital work has been undertaken by the charismatic movement. Its members have made great progress in drawing needed attention to this often misunderstood divine Person. The movement has also done remarkably well in creating a greater awareness of the importance of the fruits and charisms of the Spirit in the life of each believer. Through the work of the charismatic movement, thousands of men and women have come to accept and express deliberate and intentional discipleship with Christ.

Yet not everyone feels comfortable joining or being associated with this or other vibrant movements in the Church. I remember the first time I celebrated Mass for a community of charismatic Christians. My understanding of the gift of tongues was that it was a gift and not some sort of language that could be summoned by an individual at will. But during the Eucharistic Prayer, at the moment when I elevated the Host, the entire congregation, including the deacon serving with me at the altar, burst into tongues. I honestly didn't know what to do as I stood there holding the Eucharist in my hands. I remember looking at the Host and asking Jesus to tell me when I should place him back on the paten. It was a strange and disconcerting experience.

As a result of such however well-intentioned experiences, the Holy Spirit is too often perceived as either an anecdote of early Christianity or the property of a select or "fringe" group in the Church. In my mind, it is imperative to reintroduce the Holy Spirit to all the baptized, especially to those who have been confirmed. The rich, full, abundant life Jesus promised depends upon it.

This need to reintroduce the Holy Spirit has become clearer to me over the past ten years. Through the encouragement and blessing of my bishop, I have had the privilege of traveling throughout the United States leading parish missions and retreats. My time at a parish usually puts me in touch with the various groups and ministries found there. I am invariably asked to speak with the students preparing for the sacrament of confirmation, which I have come to regard as the most poorly presented of all the Church's sacraments.

Such was the case at a parish in Dallas where I was leading a parish mission. The director of religious education (DRE) requested that I speak to the confirmation class. While this was an unplanned appearance, it was for me a most welcome one. So on the evening I was to conclude the mission and just before my last talk, the DRE accompanied me, literally, to the "upper room"—the second floor of the parish school building—introduced me to the instructor and the students, and then turned the class over to me. That's when the fun began!

I started off by asking how many of the students really didn't want to be there that evening. I promised them they could be honest without any retribution. After a few minutes of silence, one brave young man defiantly raised his hand. He was so proud to be the first that others soon followed his lead. Eventually the truth came to light as every hand was raised. It was clear: Not one of them wanted to be there. I certainly could appreciate why for reasons that would most assuredly see me exiled by the hierarchy.

This admission by the students was exactly what I hoped for and expected. Their courageous honesty allowed me to say to them what I enjoy saying to all young people in their situation: "Since you don't want to be here, I will offer you the possibility of never having to come back to this or any religion class—ever."

At this point, I thought the DRE was going to have a stroke and that the young man teaching the class would move to throw me out the second-story window. I'm sure that, at the very least, they were rethinking their invitation that I speak to the confirmands. But before they could whisk me away, I quickly told the stunned students what I wanted them to do.

"When you go home this evening, respectfully ask your parents or guardians one simple question. If they can't answer the question, you are not obligated ever to return. The question I want you to ask is this: 'Mom, Dad, Grandma, Grandpa, what difference has confirmation made in your life?'" Knowing that this question might make their parents uncomfortable, I suggested substituting it with another: "What difference does Jesus make in your life?"

The room was utterly silent. Every person in that room was looking at me in shock, disbelief, or confusion. I certainly held everyone's attention, if for no other reason than the fact that they were all thinking, "This priest is crazy!"

I continued by telling them that if they were not comfortable asking their parents, they could ask the DRE, their religion teacher, or even their pastor. My reason was simple: If the people responsible for teaching the faith can't explain the difference faith makes, then faith makes no difference. If those who have been confirmed can't explain on a personal level why the sacrament is necessary, then it really isn't. It becomes just another thing one does because one is Catholic.

No one in the room that evening knew quite what to do. My approach to religious education went well beyond what any of them had ever experienced. After another few minutes of silence, one brave boy raised his hand. Looking directly at him, I said, "I know what you're going to ask me. You want to know what difference confirmation and Jesus make in my life."

He enthusiastically nodded his head in agreement. He thought he had caught me off guard, but I jumped right in with my ready answers to the initial question as well as its substitute. For the next hour we were all engaged in the greatest of discussions, in which even their instructor and the DRE participated. Imagine, a room full of Catholics talking to each other about the importance of Christ in their lives!

By the end of our time together, the young people were excited about the sacrament for which they were preparing. Some weeks later I heard from the pastor (he had been asked the question by most of the students), that every student returned to the class the following week and every week thereafter. At their invitation, I flew back to be with them on their special day.

The reason I enjoy asking people this question—and why I encourage those learning about the faith to do the same— is because, like St. Peter, I think that anyone claiming to be a follower of Christ should be always ready with an explanation as to why. This explanation must issue from the heart and not the head. After all, one can recite all the truths of the Catholic faith or even be an astute theologian but not know the Person of Christ.

Being ready to give an explanation for our hope requires our being able to express to someone the real, tangible significance of Jesus and the sacraments, first and foremost from the context of our lives and not as memorized statements from the *Catechism*. If someone is interested enough to ask us what we believe and why, our answers should always resonate with the vitality of our lived experience.

I met Jesus on a Thursday afternoon in June when I was nine years old; that experience changed my life. I know that many Catholics—including some ordained ministers of the Church— are unaccustomed to talking about the faith in this way, preferring to use lofty, impersonal concepts of theology and the ethical norms that flow from them. All I can say is that the teachings of the Catholic faith didn't save my life; Jesus did.

Only through the Holy Spirit do we find the freedom to answer such questions within the context of our lived relationship with Christ. Without the invigorating presence of the Spirit in our lives, Jesus would be just an abstraction and our faith an ethical program—at best. It is the Spirit who makes an encounter with Christ possible, and it is the Spirit who sustains that encounter. Living the richness of our Catholic faith depends wholly upon the vitalizing presence of the Spirit. This won't necessarily entail waving our hands in the air, singing lively songs of praise and worship, or falling "slain" to the floor of our parish churches (although it might). It simply means that we come to know and respond to this Gift of the Father and the Son.

The men St. Paul met at Ephesus had the whole of their lives changed the day they received the Holy Spirit. What began in baptism was completed when Paul laid his hands upon them and invoked the Spirit, who then came on them. The life of every confirmed member of the Church has changed in the same way. The reason why many don't know this is because they do not know the Spirit.

It is my hope that the following will help to change that. The Holy Spirit may be the most forgotten member of the Trinity, but he is the ever-present member. The Spirit is the bond uniting us with the Father and the Son, an always accessible Gift who longs to fill us with the love of the Trinity.

CHAPTER ONE

The Holy Spirit in the Life of the Trinity

Indeed, even though there are so-called gods in heaven and on earth (there are, to be sure, many "gods" and many "lords"), yet for us there is
one God, the Father,
    from whom all things are and for whom we exist,
and one Lord, Jesus Christ,
    through whom all things are and through whom we exist.
But not all have this knowledge. (1 Corinthians 8:5–7)

The Catholic Church professes that Jesus has revealed God, the Creator of all that exists, as a relationship of divine Persons whose eternal, loving communion answers the most penetrating questions about human existence, meaning, purpose, and destiny. The mystery of the Holy Trinity is therefore the very heart of Christianity, the origin of everything the Church teaches and all that she does. And yet, St. Paul's words to the Christians of Corinth reflect the difficulties inherent in trying to explain the concept of "one God in three persons" (CCC 253). Among all the prevailing "gods" and many "lords," why did the Church insist upon such a radical notion of God?

The answer is firmly grounded in the lives of the apostles, the men who were historical eyewitnesses of Christ. They repeatedly heard Jesus identify both his mission and his Person with the Father. In fact, before Jesus departed from this world, he went so far as to tell the apostles, "Whoever has seen me has seen the Father" (John 14:9).

In spreading the Good News, the apostles preached about the nature of God according to their experience. Jesus had persistently told them that he never speaks or acts on his own; he does only the things his Father tells him to do. He had gradually broadened their understanding of the God of Israel. In time they too could do not only the works that Jesus does but even greater ones. Among these greater works would be the revelation of God as a Trinity of divine Persons.

A New Conception of God

In order that this mission of carrying on the works of Jesus might take place, these chosen eyewitnesses needed the help of "another Advocate." Jesus promised that the Father would send this Advocate at Jesus's request. He would teach them all things and remind them of everything Jesus had taught them. He would embolden them to preach about the God they had come to know through the Son. As a gift from the Father and the Son, the Holy Spirit would ensure the accurate content of Christ's message and its faithful transmission by the apostles and their successors.

God, who spoke in the past, continues to converse with us, the Church, the Spouse of his beloved Son. And the Holy Spirit, through whom the living voice of the Gospel rings out in the Church—and through her in the world— leads believers to the full truth, and makes the Word of Christ dwell in them in all its richness. (CCC 79, quoting *Dei Verbum* 8.3, see Colossians 3:16; CCC 77, 78).

After the outpouring of the Holy Spirit at Pentecost, the apostles traveled great distances, proclaiming the God whose love for humanity had been definitively revealed through the life, death, resurrection, and exaltation of Jesus, a man they knew to be God. This message would prove to be "a stumbling block to Jews and foolishness to Gentiles" (1 Corinthians 1:23). Yet no matter the difficulties, the early Church couldn't talk about God without talking about Jesus and his death on the cross.

The apostles and their successors were convinced that only in an encounter with Jesus and the acceptance of his love could the fatherhood of God be truly known and experienced. They preached "the Gospel," because God has destined all humanity for "adoption to himself through Jesus Christ, in accord with the favor of his will." For the apostles, preaching Jesus meant preaching the Father.

Unfortunately, as the Church grew and spread, conflicting claims about the nature and Person of Jesus negatively impacted the way people thought about God. Thus, in order to affirm once and for all the true teaching of the apostles, the first "ecumenical" gathering of bishops (that is, bishops "from the whole world") was held in Nicaea. It was here that the Fathers of the Church together affirmed "that the Son is 'consubstantial' with the Father, that is, one only God with him" (CCC 242). They hoped that by promulgating a simple confession of faith—a creed—they could eventually dispel all prevailing distortions about the nature and identity of Jesus. This would allow future ecumenical councils to articulate more clearly the true nature of God in the dogma of the Holy Trinity.

By promulgating the Creed, the first council of bishops in Nicaea decisively affirmed what the early Christian community had long celebrated in word and sacrament: Jesus as the "refulgence of his glory, the very imprint of his being" (Hebrews 1:3). They further asserted that "the revealed truth of the Holy Trinity has been at the very root of the Church's living faith" from the earliest days of Christianity (CCC 249) and remains the heart of apostolic preaching. This is why we confess each week:

> I believe in one Lord Jesus Christ,
> the Only Begotten Son of God,
> ...
> Light from Light,
> true God from true God,
> begotten, not made, consubstantial with the Father...
> (Niceno-Constantinopolitan Creed)

By our profession, we make our own the faith preached by the apostles. We acknowledge that the Word that was with God in the beginning has come into the world with knowledge that

4

transcends even the loftiest and most sophisticated ideas about the mystery of God.

Jesus, by "taking the form of a slave" (Philippians 2:7), manifested in time exactly who he is for all eternity. This unprecedented and unrepeatable revelation began the moment Jesus was conceived in the womb of Mary. She allowed the Holy Spirit to overshadow her life so that our salvation through Jesus could be revealed to man (Colossians 1:26). Jesus, who is God incarnate came into the world so that all people might see and know the human face of God and thereby be "caught up in love of the God we cannot see" (CCC 477, quoting the *Roman Missal*, Preface of Christmas I).

In the course of handing on all that they learned and experienced with Jesus, the apostles necessarily spoke of the Spirit of God in a bold new way. On the night before he died, Jesus had spoken with them about the Holy Spirit in the language of relationship, clearly distinguishing the Spirit with the personal pronoun "he." Just as the only begotten Son has always been one with God, so has the Holy Spirit, whom the Father will send in Jesus's name (John 14:26). Although the Spirit is distinct from the Father and the Son, each remains wholly in one another.

Therefore the Father, Son, and Spirit together describe the mystery of God's life as it has always been. The unity or oneness of God was not divided into three parts by the incarnation of the Son or the sending of the Holy Spirit. Rather, the Son and the Holy Spirit together show us who God has always been. "The whole history of salvation is identical with the history of the way and the means by which the one true God, Father, Son, and Hoy Spirit, reveals himself to men 'and reconciles and unites with himself those who turn away from sin'" (CCC 234, quoting *General Catechetical Directory*, 47).

In discussing the Trinity as the "source of all the other mysteries of faith" (CCC 234), the Church continues to make use of two distinct but interrelated approaches. The first, "theology," focuses on the life of God within the Trinity, while the second, "economy," pertains to "all the works by which God reveals himself and communicates his life" (CCC 236). From her earliest days, the Church has maintained the reciprocal relationship between God's works and his inner life. God's works reveal who he is in himself, while the mystery of his inner life broadens and strengthens our understanding of all his works.

In order to shed greater light on this, the Church holds that the totality of God's works (referred to as the "divine economy") should not be considered independently of one another. They are undertaken in common by the three divine Persons but carried out in a way that is proper to each. Thus the one God's act of salvation can be described in the following way: The Father saves us by sending us the Son; the Son saves us by sacrificing his life on the cross; the Holy Spirit saves us by sanctifying us with the gift of divine life.

Although the hidden life of God remains a mystery inaccessible by reason alone, professing God as Trinity is not meant to distance us from him. Through the Son's incarnation and the sending of the Holy Spirit, not only are we capable of understanding the eternal relationship of intimate loving communion that is the Holy Trinity, we are able to share in it. This is why we were created, why every human heart cries out to be loved. This is why people discover themselves in the words of Jesus and leave everything to follow him. The revelation of God as a relationship explains what it means to be human.

The Action of the Spirit in the Old Testament

While evidence of the Trinity can be detected in the account of Creation and throughout the Old Testament, it is only through the Incarnation that this truth of God is made known. As was noted above, the Church proclaims this truth throughout the world by the gift of the Holy Spirit, who continues to take what belongs to Jesus and declare it to his followers—just as the Spirit did with the apostles. Like the "mighty wind" that hovered over the waters "when God created the heavens and the earth" (Genesis 1:1–2), the Holy Spirit hovers over the Church, lavishing gifts of grace from the God who is love.

By proclaiming and explaining the hidden life of God, the Church draws together the different ways the "Spirit of God" was described in the Old Testament. Since the name of God could not be spoken, the sacred authors would often refer to God according to his attributes. Thus, referring to the "Spirit of God" became a common way of describing God's power active in a variety of ways, such as in history, in nature, and in the universe as a whole. This affirmed the sacred authors' belief not only that God is present in the world but, more importantly, that he is interested and involved.

This is especially true with respect to bringing forth life and maintaining it. When God created mankind he gave us his own breath of life, thereby establishing an innate bond between human beings and the One who created all things. Our existence depends upon the Creator, whose breath ("spirit") formed us according to God's own divine image. As long as the breath of God" remains in us, we have life, and when it departs from us, we return to the earth from which we came.

The word for "breath" (*ruach* in Hebrew) is the same word used by the sacred authors to describe God's spirit. It should be no surprise, then, that the resurrected Jesus will breathe on his disciples and say, "Receive the holy Spirit" (John 20:22). By this sacred gesture, Jesus will impart divine life in a way that echoes the creation of man and woman from the book of Genesis. Every time we breathe in and out, we should be mindful of the God who holds our souls in his hand, the God by whose Spirit we too breathe in communion with the Father and the Son.

In the Old Testament, the Spirit of God was also responsible for the work of God in the deeds of specially chosen individuals. Through the Spirit's presence in the lives of such men and women, God acted deliberately within history on behalf of his chosen people. Such a man was Joseph, the great-grandson of Abraham. This one whom Jacob loved "best of all his sons" (Genesis 37:3) was sold to the Ishmaelites by his jealous brothers (Genesis 37:25–28), eventually ending up a slave in Egypt (Genesis 37:36). Fortunately, Joseph's master, Potiphar, "saw that the Lord was with him" and put Joseph in charge of his household (Genesis 39:3–4).

Things would take a bad turn for Joseph, but amid false accusations and imprisonment, the Lord remained with him. Joseph was held in prison for two long years, until the wisdom with which he could interpret dreams garnered the attention of Pharaoh. Summoned before the ruler of Egypt, Joseph explained the dreams that had been "agitating" Pharaoh's spirit. When Joseph was finished, Pharaoh exclaimed, "Since God has made all this known to you, there is no one as discerning and wise as you are. You shall be in charge of my household, and all my people will obey your command" (Genesis 41:39–40). Pharaoh knew there was no other man in the land of Egypt endowed with the spirit of God as was Joseph.

Similar things can be said about all the great leaders of God's chosen people. Through them God was able to lavish his affection upon his people, all the while teaching them the breadth of his covenant and the depth of his promises.

Weighty responsibility was given to Moses hundreds of years after Joseph, when a new pharaoh, "who knew nothing of Joseph" (Exodus 1:8), came to power in Egypt. From the midst of a burning bush, unconsumed by the flames, God called Moses to "lead [his] people, the Israelites, out of Egypt" (Exodus 3:10). Although Moses considered himself ill-suited to the task, he nonetheless did as God commanded. With the help of his brother Aaron, he led the descendants of Abraham out of their slavery in Egypt.

The ability to reveal God's face to the people of Israel was well conveyed in the life of Moses. God spoke with Israel's greatest prophet "as a man speaks to his friend" (Exodus 33:11, *RSV*). Having such intimate friendship with God meant that Moses could communicate God's will and speak God's word purely and distinctly. Moses served the Lord by handing on to the people only that which he learned from God. However, Moses personally longed to see the day when the Lord would raise up another prophet like him.

For forty years Moses led the Israelites on their journey to "a land flowing with milk and honey" (Exodus 3:8). Almost from the start, the needs of the people and their disagreements with one another were burdensome. In order that Moses is not overwhelmed by his responsibilities, God takes some of the spirit he has conferred on Moses and bestows it upon seventy other men. This portioning of the spirit, more than a mere division of labor, enabled the men to participate in the call Moses had experienced in the desert.

When the Israelites were at last about to enter the land promised to Abraham and his descendants, the time for Moses to die was near. Before he died, Moses laid his hands upon Joshua, the young man who had been serving as Moses's aide, and bestowed on him the commission to lead the people in all things and guide them in all their actions. Joshua, filled with the "spirit of wisdom" (Deuteronomy 34:9) and knowing that God would be with him wherever he went, succeeded Moses. He led the Israelites across the Jordan River into the Promised Land.

As Abraham's descendants grew from a tribe into a nation, God consistently "stirred up the holy spirit" (Daniel 13:45) of individuals, in order to work great signs and wonders on behalf of his people. When Gideon defeated Midian, Samson destroyed the Philistines, and David felled Goliath, God alone was the source of their strength and he alone the victor.

O God, we have heard with our own ears;
 our ancestors have told us
The deeds you did in their days,
 with your own hand in days of old:
You rooted out nations to plant them,
 crushed peoples and expelled them.
Not with their own swords did they conquer the land,
 nor did their own arms bring victory;
It was your right hand, your own arm,
 the light of your face for you favored them.
(Psalm 44:2–4)

Unfortunately, Israel did not always look to the Lord for her strength and protection. God came to the help of his people even when their sinfulness caused great harm and sweeping ruin. He raised up men and women of valor to deliver Israel.

"After David, Israel gave in to the temptation of becoming a kingdom like other nations" (CCC 709). Although this failure would cause them to be held captive by other nations, it would also facilitate a shift in their hopes and expectations. The Israelites may have been forgetful of God's law and unfaithful to his covenant, yet in the midst of their ensuing suffering, God sent them prophets. These promised that the work of God's spirit would be the restoration of the kingdom. During the Exile, Israel also came to understand that God was up to something new.

Israel would once again be a kingdom, established by a shoot from the stump of Jesse. God would rest his spirit upon an heir of David. This would be a spirit of wisdom, understanding, counsel and strength—a spirit of knowledge and of fear of the Lord. With the promise of a chosen one, the hopes of the people gradually assumed more religious overtones and moved away from pleas for valiant deeds, physical strength, and special prudence.

Some prophets spoke of a messiah. With the increasing anticipation of the Messianic Age, people came to believe that the activities of the Spirit would be spread beyond Israel: All would live by God's statutes and follow his decrees. While anticipating the Spirit of grace and petition that God would pour out upon the house of David and on the inhabitants of Jerusalem, they also yearned for the day when this gift would be universally shared.

Through the gifts they received, the prophets were able to reveal the face of God as one of consolation and redemption. They thereby directed the people on the true path to the One who is the fulfillment of human destiny. The prophets were sent by God not to predict the future or calm people's fears with guarantees of physical, social, or political security. Rather, they were sent to turn the hearts of the people again toward God, toward doing "what is right and just" (Jeremiah 22:3). They were to set captives free and heal the brokenhearted.

During the time of preparation for Christ's coming, the people were called to rely on God alone and await the justice of the Messiah. They looked forward in hope:

> I give you thanks, O Lord;
>> though you have been angry with me,
>> your anger has abated, and you have consoled me.

> God indeed is my salvation;
>> I am confident and unafraid.
> for the Lord, is my strength and my might
>> and he has been my salvation. (Isaiah 12:1–2)

As expectations about the coming of the Messiah intensified, so did the desire for a new experience of the Spirit of God. Only the Spirit of God could prepare the people for the new kingdom. God would indeed save his people and pour out his Spirit upon all mankind. Joel, the ardent prophet of the Messianic Age, pointed out to the people of Israel that the hope of Moses was soon to be fulfilled, that God's Spirit would come to rest on all his people.

> Your sons and daughters will prophesy,
>> your old men will dream dreams,
>> your young men will see visions;
> Even upon your male and female servants
>> in those days, I will pour out my spirit. (Joel 3:1–2)

The Action of the Spirit in the New Testament

The prophetic texts that mention the sending of the Holy Spirit are ways by which God speaks to his people in the language of promise, love, and faithfulness. In the New Testament, these "oracles" see fulfillment, beginning with the incarnation of God's Son. They are thoroughly refined and wonderfully illuminated on the day of Pentecost, when the minds of the Lord's disciples are opened "to the understanding of [Jesus's] Death and Resurrection" (CCC 737). On that day, they come to see that the salvation for which the people of Israel longed will indeed be accomplished through the outpouring of the Holy Spirit within the context of the believing community.

Through the outpouring of the Holy Spirit at Pentecost, the community of believers is constituted as the body of Christ, the Church. The kingdom announced by Christ is thereby opened to those who believe in him, those who, by faith now share in the life of the Trinity. The gift of God's Spirit is the definitive conferral of salvation and the fulfillment of the Old Testament promises.

The movement toward this miraculous event begins with the preaching of John the Baptist, a man "filled with the holy Spirit even from his mother's womb" (Luke 1:15). While John has a rightful place with the prophets of old, he is more than a prophet. He completes the cycle of prophets and proclaims the coming of the Messiah. Through the gift of the Spirit, John completes the work of making the people ready for the Lord. He consoles Israel, bearing witness to the light.

John comes baptizing with water so that Jesus might be made known in Israel. Through this baptism for the repentance of sins, the Holy Spirit initiates the restoration of man according to the divine likeness. The Spirit will complete this work through, with, and in Christ Jesus, the Lamb of God and Son of God, who baptizes with water and the Holy Spirit. He offers men and women the experience of new birth for entrance into the kingdom of God (John 3:5).

John the Baptist made it clear that he was not the Messiah, testifying instead that he saw the Spirit descend like a dove and remain upon Jesus. This occurred at the beginning of Jesus's public ministry, after he came up out of the water. The Father and the Spirit manifested the truth that Jesus is, the Messiah.

The Spirit is the moving force behind every activity of Christ. Beginning with Jesus's forty days in the desert and his decisive battle with Satan, the Spirit is at work in Jesus's ministry. Every parable, sermon, and miracle evidence the fact that the "Spirit of the Lord" is upon him (Luke 4:18).

In the synagogue of his hometown, Jesus reads from the scroll of the prophet Isaiah and says to the assembly, "Today this scripture passage is fulfilled in your hearing" (Luke 4:21). In the power of the Holy Spirit, Jesus has come:

> To bring good news to the afflicted,
> > to bind up the brokenhearted,
> To proclaim liberty to the captives
> > release to the prisoners,
> To announce a year of favor from the Lord
> …
> To comfort all who mourn. (Isaiah 61:1–2)

The Holy Spirit is integral to the mission of Jesus. Throughout his public ministry, Jesus gradually reveals the Person of the Holy Spirit, preparing his followers to welcome this powerful presence. He appoints seventy-two disciples to precede him into every town and place he wishes to visit. Responding to the great need of the people, Jesus—like Moses before him—allows others to participate in his ministry. At his command, this large group sets out to cure the sick and preach the nearness of God's kingdom.

When the disciples have completed their task, they return overjoyed at all the things they were able to accomplish in Jesus's name.

Rejoicing in the Holy Spirit, Jesus praises the Father for every-thing he has revealed to the childlike. The disciples are blessed to have seen and heard what many kings and prophets longed to see and hear.

The revelation of the Holy Spirit reaches a new level in the Upper Room on the night before Jesus dies. Preparing his disciples for his passion and death, Jesus speaks to them of "another Advocate," "the Spirit of truth" whom the Father will send in Jesus's name. The Spirit will teach the disciples everything and remind them of all that Jesus told them. This remembrance is greater than the mere recollection of past events. These past events will permeate the disciples' ministries, so that they can faithfully transmit the correct meaning of everything Jesus said and did. The Holy Spirit guarantees the testimony of the apostles, leading them into all truth and teaching them of the things to come.

After his passion, death, and resurrection, and before returning to the Father, Jesus again speaks to the apostles about the Holy Spirit, who will come to them once Jesus has been taken from their sight. In the power of the Holy Spirit, they are to be Christ's witnesses "in Jerusalem, throughout Judea and Samaria, and to the ends of the earth."

This fundamental gift of the Holy Spirit—whom Jesus called the "promise of the Father"—was given to the apostles at Pentecost. And in the miraculous events that accompanied the sending of the Holy Spirit, it became quite clear that the saving action of God would compellingly move forward. Those present in the Upper Room were recreated according to the order of grace to share the life of God, who is love. They were able to, as it were, "breathe with God."

This love poured into their hearts by the Holy Spirit is no mere human sentiment but the indwelling presence of the divine. It courses through them as gently and imperceptibly as the air they breathe. This new life they receive from the Holy Spirit enables them to observe all that Jesus has commanded, because by it they are grafted into the life of Jesus—like branches to a vine (John 15:5).

From this day onward the Holy Spirit will lead and guide the Church and be the source of inspiration for all those who accept with faith God's continuing action in human history. The Holy Spirit is the unseen power that fuels the ministry and activity of the apostles and gives them the courage to speak in Jesus's name, even when facing men of power who would like to silence them (Acts 4:1–21). Thus does the Holy Spirit fulfill in them Jesus's earlier promise that they would never have to be anxious over what they are to say in times of persecution.

With the consolation of the Holy Spirit, the Church will grow in numbers, and many people throughout all of Judea, Galilee, and Samaria will be added to Jesus's many followers. Perhaps recalling the commissioning of the seventy-two, the apostles appoint "seven reputable men, filled with the Spirit and wisdom" (Acts 6:3) to assist them in the care of the growing Christian community. Again like Moses, who centuries before laid hands upon Joshua, the apostles pray and then lay hands upon these men chosen to serve.

Just as the Holy Spirit guides the apostles in their decision to appoint deacons, the Spirit also moves prophets and teachers in the church at Antioch to set apart Barnabas and Saul to preach to the Gentiles. Beginning in Cyprus, they eventually venture to Asia and Europe. Paul, a man who once persecuted the followers of Jesus, becomes a great missionary evangelist and writes the most comprehensive and impressive testimony to the Spirit.

Although Paul is truly filled with the Holy Spirit, it is impossible to define exactly what the word *Spirit* (*pneuma* in Greek) means to him. Paul's usage of this Greek word covers a wide field with sharp contrasts. St. Paul does not invent the functions he ascribes to the Holy Spirit but rather explicates what was being experienced within the life of the believing community. He seeks to describe in an orderly fashion the amazing variety of ways the Spirit affects us, recounting the God-given blessings—or gifts—of being baptized with water *and* the Holy Spirit.

One of the most striking and surprising gifts of the Spirit that St. Paul describes is the gift of tongues, an incomprehensible, animated stammering of faith in praise of God. While Paul presents this phenomenon in a mostly favorable light, he also demands that it be exercised in an orderly way and only for the building up of the Church. He insists that the functions of the Holy Spirit should never be restrained (1 Thessalonians 5:19–21) and at the same time points out that the Holy Spirit works for unity and order.

St. Paul also mentions several gifts of the Spirit that are superior to the enthusiastic outbursts of tongues. The most important of these is inspired prophecy, by which Paul means the explanation of the word of God for the effective edification of the community. Just as in the days of the old covenant, the gift of prophecy is not given to predict the future but rather to point people toward a deeper understanding of the God who is their destiny.

It is clear from his depictions and characterizations of the Holy Spirit that St. Paul regarded the Spirit as the fulfillment of the Old Testament promises. Through the dynamic presence of the Holy Spirit, the members of Christ's body experience a foretaste of final salvation. The resurrection of Christ, which the disciples experienced, was not to be thought of as the consummation of all things in his Person. St. Paul came to see that there might be a long span of time between Jesus's resurrection and his return in glory. He knew that the Lord would return at an unknown time, like a thief in the night.

During this interval, the Spirit is ever present to the Church, even when it is not gathered together for worship: He is active in the everyday life of the faithful. As the foundation for a totally new life and activity, the Holy Spirit keeps alive a sense of dependence on God and encourages each believer to live in imitation of Christ. The Spirit is active not only in the passing moments of religious ecstasy but everywhere and always in the life of the baptized, who have become temples in which God dwells. Through the Person of the Holy Spirit, the whole Church and each member can not only express their thanks and joy to God but also, most importantly, call God Father, just as Jesus did.

The Identity and Ministry of the Holy Spirit

The different functions of the Holy Spirit enumerated by St. Paul serve as a foundation on which the early Church Fathers slowly (and at times with some controversy) constructed a theology of the Spirit. Near the end of the fourth century, St. Augustine furthered these efforts by writing an influential treatise on the Holy Trinity

(*De Trinitate*). In it, he uses one of his cherished passages from St. Paul's Letter to the Romans to offer new insights about the identity of the Holy Spirit. Focusing on the Spirit as gift and the Spirit as love, Augustine references Paul's passionate assertion that the love of God has been poured into our hearts "through the Holy Spirit that has been given to us" (Romans 5:5).

Augustine further advances the notion of the Holy Spirit as gift by recalling the words Jesus spoke to the woman at the well in Samaria: "If you knew the gift of God and who is saying to you, 'Give me a drink,' you would have asked him and he would have given you living water" (John 4:10). This "living water" is none other than the Holy Spirit, which will be given to and will enlighten all those who come to believe in Jesus.

Fortunately, St. Augustine knew that it wasn't enough to simply affirm that the Holy Spirit is truly the gift of God. He understood that people often want to know exactly what a particular gift is, well before receiving it. For Augustine, this explains why Jesus spent a substantial part of his public ministry explaining this gift his followers would receive once he had returned to his Father. Linking together Jesus's words with those of St. Paul, Augustine shows that the Holy Spirit is truly the gift God wishes to lavish upon us, because the Holy Spirit is in fact God. The apostles didn't receive some *thing* from God; in the Person of the Holy Spirit, they received God himself!

This explains why Jesus referred to the Holy Spirit as "living water." The Spirit has been sent by the Father precisely to bestow on us the very life of God. Through the power of the Holy Spirit, the human family is given the opportunity of being recreated according to the divine likeness, in order to share God's glory. What was forfeited through sin is now given to men and women as a gift from the Father, through Jesus his Son, in the Person of the Holy Spirit.

Those who accept the gift of the Spirit do not participate in God's life in an impersonal or external way but rather in the way of God's own Son. To paraphrase the words of St. John, "We are God's children *now!*" (1 John 3:2, emphasis added). Although it is almost too much to consider, the Holy Spirit actually adopts us into the life of God, as if we too were "God from God, light from light, true God from true God." This is how comprehensively the Father wishes us to share in his life.

We are destined to be in the Son just as he is in the Father and the Father in him, so that we may be one just as they are one. We are real members of the divine family. By the power of the Holy Spirit, we have been, as it were, "assumed" into the exclusive, total, reciprocal, and fruitful loving communion that is the Holy Trinity. The Holy Spirit will actually take what belongs to Jesus and declare it to us (John 16:14). Talk about a gift!

The penetrating insights of St. Augustine place before the Christian community the proposition that, in the Person of the Holy Spirit, the giver and the gift are the same. The Spirit, sent by Jesus and the Father, bestows divine life by utterly giving us his own life. This is the only way that a true, full, and rich experience of God is possible. That is why Jesus told his followers that he had to go or the Spirit could not come to them. Without the sending of the Spirit, their knowledge of Jesus and the Father would remain forever incomplete. It would be as partial and various as the ways God spoke in the past to his people.

By the willingness of the Holy Spirit to "hand himself over," we have the opportunity to become acquainted with the Father and the Son just as they are acquainted with each other. When Jesus told his disciples that he had come to show them the Father, he had something far greater in mind than fascinating firsthand anecdotes about the Creator of the universe. Jesus wants his followers to know the Father just as Jesus knows him. Only the Holy Spirit can make possible such a revelation, such a comprehensive sharing of self. While the Incarnation has ensured a historical dimension to this revelation, the record of Jesus's words and deeds are not capable of presenting the Person of the Father as he longs for us to know him. This underlies Jesus's insistence about having to leave his followers despite the grief it will cause them.

The Holy Spirit, because he proceeds from the Father and the Son, is the most suitable means of understanding love of the Father and the Son. He is sent to form Christ in us, that Jesus might dwell within us and give us his mind and heart.

The Holy Spirit accomplishes the revelation of God in all those who through faith have opened their lives to everything Jesus wishes to reveal. The Holy Spirit doesn't simply illuminate the mind to see the truth of Jesus's words and the meaning of his deeds; the Spirit opens the very being of the believer to experience God in a genuine encounter of love. The revelation of God happens within: It is an all-encompassing recognition that one now participates in the same loving communion as that of God's Son.

While this may be terrifying to consider, it is nonetheless the truth to which Jesus came to testify. The Father longs to speak and relate to us as one friend speaks and relates to another. And within the context of this interior revelation fired by the Holy Spirit, we are able to fully know Jesus as the Father and the Spirit know him.

The word *gift* is therefore perfectly suited to describe the identity of the Holy Spirit. Proceeding from the Father and the Son, the Holy Spirit's existence is the self-giving that eternally transpires between the two; it is the personification of all that the Father and Son want for us. This leads St. Augustine to portray the identity of the Holy Spirit as the bond of the loving communion of the Father and the Son, the guarantee that their love will never be closed in on itself. In other words, the Holy Spirit allows the Trinity to move outside itself as an outpouring of the love and grace that is God's innermost nature. This "outpouring of love" explains Creation, lies at the heart of humanity's redemption, is the reason we can know God, and is, of course, the mission of the Holy Spirit.

By accepting the identity of the Holy Spirit as gift-love (which I propose as two ways of looking at the one Spirit of God), there is little difficulty in appreciating why the Spirit has been sent into the world. The love of the Father and the Son longs to be shared. Their mutual and reciprocal giving of self to one another is generous and effusive. God is whole and complete in himself; this loving openness defines the Person of the Holy Spirit as the generous gift of divine life. For all eternity, the Spirit remains the most unthinkable and abundant love, without limit or equal. It is the ultimate love, a participation in the life of the Trinity, to which we are all called.

CHAPTER TWO

The Holy Spirit in the Life of Christ

Then Jesus came from Galilee to John at the Jordan to be baptized by him. John tried to prevent him, saying, "I need to be baptized by you, and yet you are coming to me?" Jesus said to him in reply, "Allow it for now, for thus it is fitting for us to fulfill all righteousness." Then he allowed him. After Jesus was baptized, he came up from the water and behold, the heavens were opened [for him], and he saw the Spirit of God descending like a dove [and] coming upon him. And a voice came from the heavens, saying, "This is my beloved Son, with whom I am well pleased." (Matthew 3:13–17)

*J*esus spent the first years of his life with Mary and Joseph. Much of what happened during those years remains hidden. What little has been preserved and handed on to us concerns the way in which Jesus came into the world and the reason why.

Jesus was conceived in his mother's womb by the power of the Holy Spirit, to "save his people from their sins" (Matthew 1:21). Mary and Joseph knew the truth about Jesus and provided him a home, in which he grew in "wisdom and age and favor before God and man" (Luke 2:52). The home in Nazareth was a kind of school in which Jesus was educated before undertaking the ministry for which he had been born into the world.

The dramatic and extraordinary events surrounding Jesus's birth and childhood eventually gave way to a composed and ordinary family life. When the right time had come, God the Father called his Son to leave the loving environs of his home in Nazareth and go out into the world to ransom sinners, so that we might receive adoption into the family of God.

The movement toward the public ministry of Christ seems almost the inverse of the movement of God in the account of Creation. In the opening chapter of the book of Genesis, God rests after what is described as six days of calling into being the created order. Jesus, on the other hand, emerges from his "rest" in Nazareth to undertake a new creation (CCC 374).

We are told of nothing extraordinary to mark this departure. In fact, John the Baptist seems utterly surprised to see Jesus come to the River Jordan, calling attention to the arrival of the Lamb of God, who takes away the sin of the world. The Gospels present Jesus as moving from the anonymity of his hidden years in Nazareth toward the recognition of a voice from heaven.

The Holy Spirit and the Baptism of Jesus

The voice that comes from the heavens is the Father's response to what Jesus is willingly undertaking. Placing himself with sinners— prostitutes, soldiers, and tax collectors—Jesus makes no claim of superiority and draws little attention. Here he is already showing himself to be the Lamb of God, taking upon himself the sins of the world. Jesus presents himself at the Jordan ready to assume the Father's mission, anticipating his death. The "suffering servant" foretold by the prophet Isaiah freely steps into the waters of the Jordan, sanctifying the water that will become for us the source of all righteousness.

How remarkable the scene! After all the others had been baptized, John, in spite of his own unworthiness, nonetheless watches Jesus step into the Jordan in great humility. Love brings Jesus to this moment with John, a love similar to that which brought Mary to visit John's mother, Elizabeth. This is the same love that caused John to leap with joy in his mother's womb (Luke 1:41).

Should there be any doubt that love explains the meeting of these two men, there occurs what St. John Paul II calls "a Trinitarian theophany"—an expression of the inner life of God.

> After Jesus was baptized, he came up from the water and behold, the heavens were opened [for him], and he saw the Spirit of God descending like a dove [and] coming upon him. And a voice came from the heavens, saying, "This is my beloved Son, with whom I am well pleased." (Matthew 3:16–17)

What took place that day points toward the fact that everything Jesus undergoes to save his people from their sins will be carried out through the dynamic presence of the Holy Spirit. Through their impenetrable bond as Trinitarian Persons, the same Spirit that enabled the Word to take flesh in the womb of the Virgin Mary accompanies Jesus into the water. This impenetrable union of being enables the Spirit to enter into human history with the incarnate Son as a vibrant, active force. The Holy Spirit hovering over Jesus and the waters of the Jordan calls to mind the breath of the Spirit sweeping over the waters when God first spoke creation into being.

It is clear from all four Gospels that Jesus's immersion in the waters is not undertaken alone. His flesh is the means by which the Holy Spirit permeates the created order, sanctifying the water for all those who will yearn to be united to Christ through his death and resurrection. Here where John baptizes, the Holy Spirit appears as a sign of the Father's openness to creation and history, his desire to save all men from their sins.

While Christianity takes its identity from the saving events of Jesus Christ, Jesus hasn't come on his own; he has come in the power of the Holy Spirit. The Spirit of God present in Creation and in the history of Israel, the Spirit given partially to the prophets, dwells in Jesus in absolute fullness. The whole of the Christian Scriptures testifies that Jesus is a man filled with the fullness of the Holy Spirit.

As we learn from John the Baptist, Jesus does not come to the Jordan River an unexpected savior but rather as the fulfillment of a long process of preparation, of which John himself is a vital part. John is not only a prophet but also a messenger of the Messiah, who will come in the power of the Holy Spirit in order to bring the Holy Spirit. What John foretells is validated when the voice comes from heaven: "This is my beloved Son, with whom I am well pleased" (Matthew 3:17).

The accounts of Jesus's baptism emphasize the importance of the relationship between his flesh and the Holy Spirit. The incarnate Son is the Christ, the anointed one, and his historical presence should never be considered apart from his anointing. The Gospel writers use every aspect of Jesus's life to link his mission with his possession of the Holy Spirit. From his virginal conception to his resurrection from the dead, Jesus operates out of the fullness of the Holy Spirit.

At the beginning of Jesus's public ministry, it is clear that the true identity of Jesus cannot be considered apart from the Holy Spirit. The man who comes to the waters of the Jordan River is no mere man; he is the incarnate Son of the Father on whom the Spirit eternally rests. He has come

> to bring glad tidings to the poor,
> ...
> ...to proclaim liberty to captives
>   and recovery of sight to the blind,
>   to let the oppressed go free,
> and to proclaim a year acceptable to the Lord. (Luke 4:18–19)

Jesus has come to gather his people into a new life in the Spirit.

The Holy Spirit and the Revelation of the Father

The incarnate Son of the Father, together with the Holy Spirit, has come into the world as the revelation of the Father's presence and of his plan to redeem the human family. This plan begins to unfold immediately following Jesus's baptism. The evangelists tell us that Jesus returns from the Jordan and is "led by the Spirit into the desert to be tempted by the devil" (Matthew 4:1). Mark says that "the Spirit drove him" (Mark 1:12). This mysterious event is a fitting prelude to Jesus's wondrous ministry.

Living among wild beasts, eating nothing, and being cared for by angels, Jesus shows us how his entire being, indeed his very identity, is rooted in his relationship with the Father. Satan tries three times to have Jesus renounce this relationship, to have him compromise his relationship with God. Unlike Adam in Paradise and the people of Israel during their forty years in the desert, Jesus shows himself to be the new Adam who fulfills his vocation perfectly. Jesus conquers Satan by remaining absolutely obedient to the Father's will, demonstrating that he truly is God's servant.

Jesus's responses to the temptations he faces reveal just what it means to say that he is the Anointed One sent by God. Through the Love that binds his life with the Father, the Love with which he is anointed, Jesus is utterly secure in having come into the world as a man. He lives on every word that comes forth from the mouth of God. Jesus refuses to put God to the test and is wholly dedicated to God's service. With the strength of the Holy Spirit, Jesus crushes Satan—not just for himself but for us. He is not a high priest unable to sympathize with our weaknesses, but one who has similarly been tested in every way, yet has never succumbed to sin.

Through these tests in the desert, the revelation of the Father begins to unfold. No wonder the devil leaves, though still hoping there will come a better time to lead Jesus astray.

After vanquishing Satan in the desert, Jesus returns to Galilee, proclaiming the Gospel and the time of fulfillment. Now the work of revealing the Father unfolds in earnest, as Jesus sets out to establish the kingdom of heaven on earth, so that men and women might share in divine life. The work of redemption is begun. In the power of the Holy Spirit, Jesus will establish this kingdom and reveal the One who reigns over it.

The kingdom of God is unlike any earthly realm. It is not a place or territory; it is not bound by any borders. It is universal in scope, intended for people of all nations. The kingdom of God is not an abstract idea or merely a creative way of describing the unimaginable. Rather it is the ultimate reality.

The kingdom Jesus announces is the relationship he shares with the Father, from which the Holy Spirit proceeds as an ineffable expression. In order to build concretely the communion of life and love that will rule, order, and guide God's kingdom, Jesus immediately gathers men around himself. These are the beginning and living signs of that kingdom and the foundation of his Church.

The Spirit who led Jesus into the desert remains with him throughout his public ministry. At the sound of Jesus's words, the Holy Spirit falls upon the men Jesus invites to follow him. Although this initial reception of the Spirit is partial, the Spirit is already at work, ordering their lives according to their new purpose as fishers of men (Luke 5:10).

In order to accept Jesus's invitation to become part of the family of God, the men he calls must trust his word. It is the Spirit who provides the interior help they need. As the personified openness of God to creation and human history, the Spirit awakens in them their innate yearning for God. Through the Spirit, they are able to judge the things Jesus says in an entirely new context. They immediately leave everything to follow him, because they believe that Jesus could never deceive them.

Peter will exemplify how the Spirit works in this respect on two different but vitally important occasions: first, when he refuses to walk away after Jesus referred to himself as "the living bread that came down from heaven" (John 6:51); and second, when he confesses Jesus as "the Messiah, the Son of the living God" (Matthew 16:16). Peter comes to these conclusions through the Holy Spirit, by whom the Father's revelation is made known. "Blessed are you, Simon son of Jonah. For flesh and blood has not revealed this to you, but my heavenly Father" (Matthew 16:17).

Right from the start, this initial gathering of men is being formed into the family of God. While Jesus will always remain the heart of this gathering, the Spirit is integral to their being built up according to the pattern of Christ, their head. With every sermon and every miracle, the Holy Spirit is present to help the disciples perceive the reign of God in their midst and to strengthen their inner selves, so that Christ may dwell in their hearts through faith, and they may be grounded in love.

The words and works of Christ and the inspiration of the Spirit will culminate in the paschal mystery—Jesus's death on the cross and his resurrection. Jesus—in the Holy Spirit—prepares the way toward this unrepeatable event by which the kingdom of God will be so definitively and irrevocably established that not even the gates of hell can prevail against it When Jesus is lifted up, and when at last he hands over his spirit, he will draw all men to himself in fulfillment of the Father's plan. Through the Holy Spirit, God the Father calls all men and women into union with Christ.

The kingdom Jesus establishes in conjunction with the Holy Spirit was first announced to the children of Israel, in particular to those who returned from Exile. The hope for this messianic kingdom was held by the poor, who waited for the consolation of Israel (CCC 711). Thus, when Jesus begins his public ministry, he preaches the Good News of God's kingdom to the poor and to the little ones, while the truth remains hidden from the learned and the wise. From his birth to his death on the cross, Jesus identifies himself with the poor and lowly and shares their life. Building up this kingdom according to Jesus's teaching is the unique activity of the Holy Spirit.

Yet it is important to note that the poverty Jesus identifies as a prerequisite for entering God's kingdom should not be interpreted simply as material poverty. Those lacking in earthly goods can still be rich in heavenly ones. While watching people put their offerings in the Temple treasury, Jesus notices a "poor widow putting in two small coins" and praises her for having contributed "more than all the rest" (Luke 21:2–3). At another time, he tells his followers that material poverty will always exist. While there are many causes of material poverty and many ways to address it, the diminished condition of others should remind us of our own impoverished condition. As a result of original sin, humanity is bankrupt of the glory of God.

Fortunately, God was not content to leave us penniless. The Son is born into the world in order to adopt us into the divine family.

Jesus longs to make us heirs of something of far greater value than anything the earth, the sea, the sky, or any creature can boast. By his life, death, and resurrection, Jesus opens the way for us to claim the very source of God's wealth, God himself. He alone is the true source of the greatness of creation and all that is good and true and beautiful.

In Christ, we become heirs to the fullness of divine riches through the Holy Spirit, who is in fact this sacred trust or inheritance. We are sealed with the promised Holy Spirit, the first installment of our inheritance as God's children. Through the richness of God's grace, our humanity, once bankrupted by sin, is now united to the Creator, Redeemer, and Lord.

The kingdom of God is for the poor but only to the extent that their hearts have been humbled by the recognition of their condition. This happens to Peter when he first meets Jesus. Having listened to Jesus's teaching and experienced the miraculous catch of fish, Peter falls at Jesus's feet and begs him to leave. Peter is seized with fear because he knows himself to be a sinful man. By this humble admission of spiritual poverty, Jesus is moved to say to Peter, "Do not be afraid" (Luke 5:10). Jesus did not come to call the righteous; he came for sinners, for those who recognize their impoverished condition.

Jesus's commitment to sinners is apparent throughout his public ministry—most dramatically in the company he keeps. He repeatedly dines in the homes of sinners, calling them to a conversion that will culminate in their dining at the table in God's kingdom. When his socializing with sinners is called into question, Jesus tells the story of the lost sheep to illustrate the unfathomable joy in heaven over a sinner who repents. To all of us who forsake the fleeting treasures of the world, Jesus freely offers the wealth of the Father's boundless mercy in the Person of the Holy Spirit. The great proof of this invaluable gift of divine life and love will be the free sacrifice of his life for the forgiveness of sins.

The invitation to enter God's kingdom demands from each of us a radical choice. We must give to God everything we possess—everything that possesses us—before we can truly follow Christ. Jesus cultivates the nature of this choice through the use of parables that, at their core, contain the secret of the presence of the kingdom in this world. In order to receive these secrets, we must become disciples of Christ, allowing our lives to be good soil in which God's Word can take lasting root.

Jesus complements his words with many mighty deeds and wonders, all through the power of the Holy Spirit. They show to those with eyes to see that the kingdom is present in him, and thus they confirm that he is the promised Messiah. His works also bear witness to his having been sent by the Father. Jesus asks his followers to believe in him or in the works themselves, which are not meant to satisfy people's curiosity but rather to strengthen their faith in him. Although at times people take offense at Jesus's miracles, these miracles are meant to be signs of Jesus's anointing.

These messianic signs—by which individuals are freed from the earthly evils of hunger, injustice, illness, and death—are not meant to suggest that Jesus has come to eradicate all earth's evils. The miracles are evidence of his having come to free us from the gravest of all evils, sin—which is the fundamental cause of every form of human bondage. Sin is the reason why all creation groans in labor while it awaits the revelation of the children of God.

As mentioned earlier, at the beginning of his public life, Jesus gave the men he had chosen the first fruits of the Spirit and sent them to proclaim the kingdom of God and to heal. Jesus gradually and carefully alludes to the Holy Spirit in teaching the multitudes, in speaking with Nicodemus, in guiding the Samaritan woman, and in celebrating with others the Feast of Tabernacles. Yet with his disciples, he speaks openly of the Spirit in the context of prayer and with respect to the witness they will bear. Jesus prepares them for the full revelation of the Holy Spirit, which will happen when Jesus has been glorified through his death and resurrection, when the promises made to their fathers is fulfilled.

At that time, the Spirit of truth, the other Paraclete, will be given by the Father in answer to Jesus's prayer. He will come in Jesus's name and from the Father's side. When the Holy Spirit comes, they will know him, and he will teach them everything and remind them of everything Christ said. The Holy Spirit will lead them into all truth; glorify Christ; convict the world about sin, righteousness, and judgment; and remain with them forever.

The Holy Spirit and the Passion of Christ

The entire momentum of Jesus's public ministry is directed toward the paschal mystery of his cross and resurrection. All of Scripture speaks to the necessity of Christ to suffer. Both before and after his Passover, Jesus interpreted the Scriptures for his followers, beginning with Moses and the prophets, explaining to them that his redemptive death is essential to God's plan. Now, once and for all, God's plan of salvation is accomplished in his Son (Hebrews 9:26).

Yet, as we saw at Jesus's baptism, he does not accomplish this work alone. The Spirit moves with Jesus toward the time when he is "handed over to the chief priests and the scribes," who in turn "hand him over to the Gentiles to be mocked and scourged and crucified" (Matthew 20:18–19). The Spirit who led Jesus into the desert to be tempted by the devil leads him up to Jerusalem to vanquish Satan for good. Jesus faces humiliation and rejection with the strength that comes from the ever-present love of the Father in the Holy Spirit. He knows that, through his death, the Spirit of his anointing will be poured out upon all mankind.

What takes place in Jerusalem at the end of Jesus's public ministry began to take shape when he first came to Galilee "filled with the Holy Spirit" (Luke 4:1). Certain Pharisees and supporters of Herod, together with priests and scribes, colluded to destroy him (Mark 3:6). They accused Jesus of blasphemy and false prophecy, religious crimes punishable by stoning.

Jesus went about Judea and the surrounding countryside doing all sorts of good works. He expelled demons, forgave people their sins, and healed many of their illnesses. In the process he became familiar with tax collectors and other public sinners, often healing on the Sabbath and presenting innovative interpretations of various precepts of the Law. All of this only fueled the fury of those who sought to do away with him.

Looking historically at the words and works of Jesus, it seems as if his anointing put him at odds with the very people to whom he had been promised. To many in Israel, Jesus seemed to act against the things that were essential to living as God's chosen people. Although Jesus emphatically stated that he had not come to abolish the law or the prophets, some people thought otherwise.

Israel's Messiah, the greatest in the kingdom of heaven, seemed to be the least and weakest among men. Like the prophets before him, Jesus was increasingly misunderstood. He came revealing the truth about the God of Abraham, Isaac, and Jacob, but his words were received as though he were out of his mind. His insistence on calling sinners to repentance only angered those who were convinced of their own righteousness. After all, who but God can forgive sins?

Even the deep respect Jesus had for the Temple was misinterpreted as a wish to see it destroyed. No matter that throughout his public ministry he preached in the Temple area; no matter that he made regular pilgrimages to Jerusalem to participate in the great Jewish feasts; no matter that he drove out merchants who had made the outer courts a place of commerce; no matter that, after his resurrection, the apostles would preserve the same reverence for the Temple.

Far from having hostility toward the Temple, Jesus went so far as to identify himself with it. Through the power and presence of the Holy Spirit, Jesus is the new Temple. He is now the definitive dwelling place of God among men. He came to reconcile fallen humanity by forgiving sins. Jesus accomplished this because he and the Father remained one through the Spirit, the bond of their love. The flesh of Christ did not separate him from the Father. Rather, because of the Spirit by which the Son took flesh, Jesus was able to do the works of his Father.

Jesus is not a man claiming to be God; nor is he a man who was made God by the Holy Spirit. Jesus, in his Person, really does make the Father of Mercies present, the Father who does not wish that anyone be lost. He hoped that the religious authorities of Jerusalem would believe in him because of the works he accomplished among them. He therefore called them to the same death to self that is required of all his followers. Unfortunately, the way in which he went about fulfilling the promises of God was too much for them to comprehend. They remained hardened in their refusal to believe and persisted in judging Jesus to be a blasphemer deserving of death.

Jesus was therefore delivered to his enemies. His tragic demise was not the result of chance or an unforeseen coincidence of historical circumstances but a part of the mystery of God's plan. By no means does this imply that those who handed Jesus over to death were "merely passive players in a scenario written in advance by God" (CCC 599; see Acts 3:13). God's eternal plan of redemption takes into account each person's free response to the grace that's offered through his Spirit. God therefore permitted the acts of violence perpetrated toward his Son in the blindness of Herod, Pontius Pilate, the Gentiles, and the people of Israel.

The Scriptures foretold that this divine plan of salvation would entail the death of the righteous one as the ransom that would free men from the slavery of sin. "Christ died for our sins in accordance with the scriptures" (1 Corinthians 15:3), and he would later explain this mystery to his disciples as they walked along the road to Emmaus (see Luke 24:27).

In Christ we have been ransomed from sin with the precious blood of Christ. From the foundation of the world, Jesus was destined to free us from the punishment of original sin, the death of the soul. God sent his own Son to save us from something far worse than biological death. God made him to be sin who did not know sin, so that in him we might have eternal life. Through the Spirit of God's only Son, we become righteous

This redeeming love that is the Holy Spirit unites Jesus and the Father. In the power of the Spirit, Jesus understands the rebelliousness caused by sin. On the cross he feels the great chasm separating humanity and the Father, but he also knows within the depths of his Sacred Heart the longing in our own hearts to be whole. Jesus perpetually lives in solidarity with us sinners, being bound to us now through the same Spirit with which he is eternally bound to the Father.

God's plan for us is one of generous, incomprehensible love. Prior to any merit on our part, God showed his love for us, in that Christ died for us while we were still sinners. The love of the Father that the Son expresses by his death on the cross excludes no one. Jesus came to give his life as a ransom for many, dying for all men without exception. This was the will of the Father.

The desire to embrace the Father's plan of redeeming love explains the whole of Jesus's life, from the first moment of the Incarnation. This love led the Lord to lay down his life for us and do all that the Father commanded him (John 14:31). The Holy Spirit was an ever comforting and encouraging presence in Jesus's human heart.

As the ultimate expression of love for the Father, Jesus willingly lays down his life of his own accord. In the sufferings Jesus endured and by his death, his humanity became the perfect instrument of the love that he shares with the Father, the love that desires the salvation of all women and men. This intentional giving of self in love was perfectly expressed during the meal he shared with the twelve apostles on the night he was betrayed. Before he died, Jesus transformed this last meal with the apostles into the memorial of his self-offering to the Father for the salvation of the world, and he asked the apostles to perpetuate it. In doing so, Jesus instituted the apostles as priests of the new covenant, so that through his flesh and blood all might substantially experience the depth of the Father's love.

The sacrifice Jesus made through, with, and in his body on the cross completes and surpasses all other sacrifices. He is truly the unblemished Paschal Lamb whose sacrifice accomplishes the definitive redemption of fallen humanity. Jesus is the sacrifice of the new covenant who reconciles us with God and at the same time restores us to communion with him. By offering his life to the Father through the Holy Spirit, Jesus becomes the perfect reparation for our disobedience. In his flesh and blood, he is both God's offering to us for the forgiveness of sins and our offering to God in thanksgiving for having been forgiven. Love to the end makes this sacrifice wholly Eucharistic, a perpetual memorial of redemption, atonement, and satisfaction.

In his loving plan of salvation, God the Father ordained that Jesus his Son should taste death for everyone. Jesus also experienced the condition of death—the separation of his soul from his body—between the time he died on the cross and the time he was raised from the tomb. We might naturally wonder about the mystery of Holy Saturday, what the horror of this day was like. Just as Christ was silenced by the reprehensible actions of Good Friday, so was the Holy Spirit in a sense rendered ineffective.

Because the Holy Spirit is the personification of the love and life of God and the means by which God extends himself to creation and to man, he must surely have been touched by the agony and disgrace of Jesus lying in the tomb. What must it have been like for the Holy Spirit to hold all things together, in the love that is his very being, on a day when the greatest of all loves lay defeated by indifference and hatred?

The Holy Spirit and Jesus's Resurrection from the Dead

The Holy Spirit remained always present to the divine Person of Christ, including the time of his death. The Spirit with whom Christ had been anointed from his birth accompanied him into the deep recesses of death, in order that new life might burst forth. The mystery of their union even unto death portends the salvation of the human family.

Jesus truly experienced death. His soul entered the realm of the dead. But unlike all others who have died, Jesus descended as Savior, bringing to imprisoned souls the Good News of God's redemptive mercy. The Scriptures refer to this dwelling place of the dead as "hell" (*Sheol* in Hebrew; *Hades* in Greek), the place whose inhabitants are deprived of the vision of God. Before the resurrection, this was the lot of all the dead, whether wicked or virtuous. While they awaited the Redeemer, they were deprived of the One who alone could give them life.

I don't mean to imply, however, that the predicament of the wicked and the virtuous was the same. In his parable of the poor man Lazarus, Jesus showed that, among the dead, there were those who had been received into Abraham's bosom. These were the souls Christ delivered when he descended into hell. Jesus did not undergo death to deliver the damned, nor to destroy hell. Rather, Jesus descended into hell "to free the just who had gone before him" (CCC 633), and he accomplished this through the Spirit who was with him.

The mission that began when the Holy Spirit led Jesus into the desert to be tempted comes to fulfillment when Jesus descends into the depths of the earth, so that the dead will hear the voice of the Son of God, bringing them to new life. Once again, it seems as if the Spirit leads Jesus to his ultimate encounter with Satan, to destroy the devil, and free those who through fear of death had been subject to slavery all their lives.

Christ willingly suffered death in order that he might take hold of the keys to death and life. Now every knee will bow to his name, which in the power of the Spirit is exalted above every other name. And every tongue will profess—with the Holy Spirit—that Jesus Christ is Lord.

The New Testament bears witness to the fact that the resurrection of the One who descended is a real event. Christ died for our sins in accordance with the Scriptures. He was buried, raised on the third day in accordance with the Scriptures, and appeared to Peter then to the rest of the apostles. St. Paul beautifully and concisely expresses the living tradition of the resurrection, which was handed on to him after his conversion. Through the gift of the Holy Spirit, Paul in turn will hand on what he received at the hands of the apostles.

Although we commonly think of the resurrection as a "Jesus event," it also manifests the boundless character of the Father's merciful love. The angelic words, "Why do you seek the living one among the dead? He is not here, but has been raised" (Luke 24:5–6), give fitting voice to the Holy Spirit, who is now and forever set loose in the world to bring to fruition the purposes for which Christ came.

The holy women to whom the angels spoke found the empty tomb an apt icon of what had mysteriously transpired. Although in itself the empty tomb does not constitute direct proof of Christ's resurrection, it is an indelible sign that Jesus did not simply return to earthly life. Why? Because Jesus is not found there! Every reminder of his death has been neatly rolled up and placed to the side. Jesus is no longer confined to space and time. Now, in his glorified body, Jesus is like the Holy Spirit, who breathes, moves, and goes where he wills.

The faith of the early Christian community was based on the witness of people who were still living among them. Jesus willed to make himself known to Mary Magdalene and the other women; to Peter, John, and the other apostles; and finally to five hundred people. Together this company of witnesses became the foundation of Christ's Church, which, like them, will continue to proclaim the resurrection as a historical fact. Jesus rose in his human body, not mystically in the minds and hearts of his followers.

This becomes clear when considering how the disciples responded to the reality of the risen Jesus. They were skeptical and even imagined they were seeing a ghost. The horror of Christ's passion had so shaken their faith that many of them did not initially believe the news. The Gospels present us with a distraught and frightened band of disciples who refused to believe the women who saw the angels at the empty tomb. On the evening of his resurrection, Jesus showed himself to the eleven and rebuked them for their unbelief and hardness of heart, because they had not believed those who saw him after the resurrection.

Faith in the resurrection will only be born under the action of divine grace through the descent of the Holy Spirit. Right up to the last appearance of the Lord, the disciples remained unbelieving, even in the midst of their joy and wonder. Their difficulty in accepting the fact that the risen body of Jesus was the same as that which was crucified was a response to the new properties exhibited in Jesus's glorified body. Jesus was not limited by space and time but presented himself how and when he willed: in the appearance of a gardener, as a fellow traveler on the road to Emmaus, and in other forms familiar to the times. With every appearance, Jesus hoped to awaken the disciples' faith in the resurrection. His glorified humanity—filled with the power of the Holy Spirit—now belongs to the divine realm of the Father. Christ is the man of heaven (1 Corinthians 15:35–50). In his risen body, he indeed prepared "a place for" his disciples, so that where he is they also may be.

Although the resurrection is an historical event verified by the empty tomb and by the apostles' encounters with the Risen Christ, it transcends and surpasses history. This is why the Risen Christ only revealed himself to his disciples, "to those who had come up with him from Galilee to Jerusalem," who "are [now] his witnesses before the people" (Acts 13:31). His resurrection "is an object of faith," an unmatched "intervention of God in creation and history" (CCC 648). The resurrection is an act of the Trinity, whereby the divine Persons act together as one but according to their own proper characteristics. The Father raises up Christ his Son, drawing the Son's humanity, including his body, into the Trinity. By his resurrection from the dead, Jesus is definitively revealed as Son of God in power according to the spirit of holiness. The Spirit gives life to Jesus's dead humanity and establishes his "glorious state of Lordship" (*CCC* 648).

By virtue of his divine power, Jesus effected his own resurrection. He willingly lays down his life in order that he might take it up again. His death and resurrection were not events that happened *to* him but events that happened *with* him. They are rightly *his* because it was Jesus who died, Jesus who was buried, and Jesus who rose on the third day. He knew that he would have to suffer much and die; it was for this that he came into the world.

The resurrection confirms all of Christ's works and teachings and fulfills both the promises of the Old Testament and the promises Jesus made during his earthly life. All truths, even those most difficult, find their fulfillment in Christ.

Jesus opens for us the way to a new life reinstated in God's grace, so that, just as Christ was raised from the dead, we too might have new life. Jesus's victory over death and our participation in grace bring about our adoption into the divine family. We have become brothers and sisters to Christ, not by nature but by the gift of grace. Through, with, and in the resurrection, we have a real share in the life of God's only Son, and so even now we are God's children. We have been swept up by Christ into the heart of divine life, so that we may "no longer live for ourselves but for Jesus, who died for us.

CHAPTER THREE

The Holy Spirit in the Life of Mary

In the sixth month, the angel Gabriel was sent from God to a town of Galilee called Nazareth, to a virgin betrothed to a man named Joseph, of the house of David, and the virgin's name was Mary. And coming to her, he said, "Hail, favored one! The Lord is with you." But she was greatly troubled at what was said and pondered what sort of greeting this might be. Then the angel said to her, "Do not be afraid, Mary, for you have found favor with God. Behold, you will conceive in your womb and bear a son, and you shall name him Jesus. He will be great and will be called Son of the Most High, and the Lord God will give him the throne of David his father, and he will rule over the house of Jacob forever, and of his kingdom there will be no end." But Mary said to the angel, "How can this be, since I have no relations with a man?" And the angel said to her in reply, "The holy Spirit will come upon you, and the power of the Most High will overshadow you. Therefore the child to be born will be called holy, the Son of God." (Luke 1:26–35)

When the time is right, the angel Gabriel is sent to Mary to announce the fulfillment of all God's promises. She is asked to conceive a son in whom the whole fullness of God will dwell in human form. In response to her question about something so wholly unimagined, the angel speaks to Mary of the Spirit of God in an entirely new way: She is told that the Holy Spirit will come upon her.

Here in Nazareth, God manifests how the mission of the Holy Spirit is always inextricably bound and directed to that of his Son. The child will be "Son of the Most High" because the Holy Spirit sanctifies Mary's womb and makes it fruitful. Through the power of the Holy Spirit, the Virgin of Nazareth conceives the eternal Son of the Father in a humanity taken wholly from her own.

From all eternity this daughter of Israel was chosen by God to be the mother of his Son. God willed that the Incarnation should be preceded by Mary's free assent. Through the Holy Spirit, who overshadows her and by whom Jesus is anointed, the life of mother and son perpetually illuminate and magnify each other. All that the Church believes and teaches about Mary is grounded in what it believes about Christ. Through him we understand just what the Father undertook—to prepare a body for his Son. In turn, we learn from Mary what it means not only to believe everything the Father tells us but also to have the Holy Spirit come upon you.

The Spirit of God and the Announcement of God's Plan

Before the angel Gabriel was sent to the Virgin of Nazareth, Mary's relationship with God was largely formed by the longing of her people for the promised Messiah. With her family, Mary is a member of a portion of the people of Israel who remained faithful to the precepts of the Law from the time of the Exile. Through the teachings of the prophets, this devout remnant of

Israel looked with hope to the geographical, political, and religious restoration of God's chosen people.

> After this I shall return
>> and rebuild the fallen hut of David;
> from its ruins I shall rebuild it
>> and raise it up again,
> so that the rest of humanity may seek out the Lord,
>> even all the Gentiles on whom my name is invoked.
> Thus says the Lord who accomplishes these things,
>> known from of old. (Acts 15:16–18)

Mary had learned the prayers and history of her people. She knew well how the Spirit of God had been at work in the lives of men and women. She knew that God had worked signs and wonders to lead the chosen people into the Promised Land and assure them of their future with him forever. Mary shared their hope that the coming Messiah would usher Israel into a new era and change the course of its history.

This longing for the restoration of Israel imbued the faithful with a genuine sense of anticipation. St. Luke describes this spirited disposition in two righteous individuals whom Mary and Joseph meet when they present the child Jesus to the Lord. Simeon and Anna spent their days in the Temple area, fasting and praying and worshiping God while awaiting the Messiah. They lived with an open expectancy regarding the fulfillment of God's plan.

Through the Spirit of God, Simeon knew that he would not die before he had seen the Messiah. Therefore, when he takes the child Jesus in his arms, he is ready to depart from the world; it is enough that his eyes behold the salvation and glory of his people. Simeon doesn't expect God to share the details about how the child Jesus will redeem Israel. He is open to however God will work through the child in his arms. Anna, meanwhile, thanks God for this child and speaks about him to all who hope for the salvation of the Lord

Like this devout man and woman, Mary too lived with a sense of anticipation. The Scriptures of her people recounted the stories of numerous men *and* women, weak and powerless, whom God called to manifest his faithfulness to his promises. Their stories fueled the hopes that kept Mary and the community to which she belonged faithful to God's covenant.

This doesn't mean that Mary, in any credible way, imagined becoming the mother of the Savior. It simply means that she lived her faith wholly open to whatever God might be up to. She responds, "May it be done to me according to your word" (Luke 1:38). Her answer to the angel Gabriel shows how well she understood the ways of the God of her ancestors. She didn't ask for details about the kingdom of her son or his rule over the house of Jacob. The God who extended the call was worthy of her trust. On that day Mary didn't become the handmaid of the Lord; she simply said aloud what had always sounded in the recesses of her heart.

> Know that the LORD is God,
>> he made us, we belong to him
>> we are his people, the flock he shepherds.
> (Psalm 100:3)

The moment Mary accepts God's call, she gives herself whole-heartedly to the Person and work of her son. By consenting to God's plan, she accepts within her own feminine humanity the fruitfulness of God's love in the Person of the Holy Spirit. The Spirit permeates her being—body and soul—and makes her the mother of God's Son. Because of her love for God and her conviction that with him all things are possible, Mary's life is ordered to the life and mission of the son she has conceived.

Every aspect of Mary's life changes because of her encounter with the angel Gabriel. In one unimaginable, unrepeatable, and unforgettable moment, everything she knew about God and herself is remarkably transformed by the Spirit who is poured into her life. In saying yes to the Father, Mary yields to grace. She is assumed into God's redemptive plan, not only for her people but for all the nations of the world. Mary breathes now with the breath of God and shares with him an unprecedented intimacy that surpasses even God's friendship with Moses. The announcement of the angel is more than a word about the coming redemption of man; it is first and foremost a revelation of the God of Abraham, Isaac, and Jacob in a bold declaration of the Holy Spirit.

Mary finds strength in the anointing of the Holy Spirit, enabling her to push her own feelings aside. The "troubling" words of the angel give way to a confidence that comes through grace, the invigorating gift of the Spirit. Mary shows how true openness to God requires death to self—to one's plans, hopes, and expectations. Mary is the first person to lose her life for the sake of Christ.

Through this strength that comes from the anointing of the Holy Spirit, Mary comprehends and experiences redemption as life!

The communion she shares now with the Father and the Son—in the Holy Spirit—enables her to understand more clearly the vision she has always had of the created order and other people. God has enriched her life with the gifts necessary to conceive his Son. Being full of grace means being intimately and deeply filled with God. As the *Catechism* puts it, "The Father blessed Mary more than any other created person 'in Christ with every spiritual blessing in the heavenly places' and chose her 'in Christ before the foundation of the world, to be holy and blameless before him in love'" (CCC 492, quoting Ephesians 1:3–4).

God did truly choose Mary, but she intentionally—of her own will—said yes to everything God was asking. She freely gave her consent because the Spirit of God encompassed her life. Mary will never question the demands of God's plan of redemptive love. At the conclusion of her time with the angel Gabriel, she has firmly resolved to offer to the Father whatever his Son will need from her in his ministry of redemption. Mary stands as the first of many believers who offer everything for Christ, their Savior. Theirs is the treasure of heaven.

Mary's acceptance of her vocation to receive in her womb the Son of God instills in her a sense of wonder. While Mary has lived in expectant openness to God's promises, now, through the work of the Holy Spirit, her understanding of God's action in the history of her people is concrete. There is now no distance between the events claimed by faith and her personal experience. God penetrates her life.

Mary's yes draws her, body and soul, into a deep connection with the Christ child. The entire created order becomes charged with an overwhelming sense of God's grandeur. Mary cries out her deep amazement:

> The Mighty One has done great things for me,
> and holy is his name. (Luke 1:49)

These words that Mary sings in the presence of her cousin Elizabeth are not born of sentiment. They issue from her entire being, because every dimension of her person resonates with the connection she now shares with Christ. This is precisely what it means to have the Holy Spirit in one's life.

Mary shows us that giving our lives to Christ requires that every physical, emotional, and spiritual urge yield to him. We are to live "not by bread alone…but by all that comes forth from the mouth of the LORD" (Deuteronomy 8:3). In the moment she conceives God's Son, Mary manifests the total giving of self that is the only way of being truly God's child.

In this complete gift of self, Mary possesses the freedom that only the Spirit effects. Her mind is able to appreciate the Scriptures of her people in an entirely new way—through the lens of the child she carries in her womb. As the child grows within her body, the Scriptures she has known and cherished will come to life in bold new ways. Mary will learn about Jesus in accordance with the Scriptures.

In Mary's contemplative exploration of God's Word, she discovers everything Jesus will need from her in order to carry out the Father's plan. The words of the ancient texts illuminate the eternal contours of the child she waits to see and touch and hold and love. Long before the Magi come, Mary has already laid her gifts at the feet of her unborn child. Like the star they follow to find the Messiah, the child is the sun around which Mary's life orbits. Her life is not governed by the elemental spirits of the universe or the laws of matter but by the Person of God, with whom her entire being is forever entwined.

Mary is a sign of the mysterious neediness of God. God has placed the future of his plan before her. She could have rebelled against the very notion that God "needed" her in order to bring his redemptive love into the world. She could have held on to reverent and time-honored notions of God that precluded his "need" to act with the consent of a creature. She might also have accepted the invitation to bear God's Son with resignation instead of with determination and interior peace.

Throughout the course of her life, Mary must have pondered God's decision to involve her—freely and without force—in his plan of redemption. Within the depths of her pure heart, she would find herself ever amazed at the ways in which divine love humbles itself before man.

The Holy Spirit in the Home at Nazareth

When the time comes for Mary to give birth to her son, the Holy Spirit has already charged her with a heightened attentiveness to what God is up to. The Spirit's presence enables her to recognize, even in what might seem insignificant, the Divine Providence. The future hope that she shares with her people is directed to the present, to the practical conditions and circumstances of her life. In them, the hand of God is at work for the salvation of his people.

This is most certainly the case with respect to Joseph, the man to whom she was already betrothed at the time of the Annunciation. He learns that she is with child, but Mary is not the one who explains what has happened in her life. Mary yields to the prompting of the Spirit to stay silent; she knows that God is at work in the life of the righteous man who has promised to house, protect, and care for her. With the utmost humility, Mary refrains from taking hold of the situation herself. She allows the Lord, in his own way, to quiet the anxious concerns of this upright man of the house of David.

So it happens that an angel of the Lord comes to Joseph in a dream, to inform him that the child in Mary's womb is the fulfillment of all God's promises. Joseph should therefore not be afraid to take the mother and child into his home, just as he has planned, in order to fulfill what the Lord had said through his prophets. Much like the apostles, who will immediately abandon everything and follow Jesus, Joseph awakens and immediately accepts the part he is to play by welcoming Mary into his home. His life, like hers, is now intertwined with Christ and his mission from the Father. Together they will experience that mission unfolding, with a distilled sense of wonder and with attentiveness to what God asks of each of them.

Mary and Joseph are astonished by the people they encounter and the things they hear concerning Jesus. They quickly learn how extensively God's plan punctuates the ordinary and expected aspects of life with the most extraordinary and unexpected signs of his presence. At the birth of Jesus, for example, the shepherds recount to his mother and Joseph the amazing things the angel has shared with them concerning Jesus. The Magi come from distant lands and prostrate themselves before the child in homage (Matthew 2:11). When Mary and Joseph go to the Temple to fulfill the requirements of the Law, God punctuates this customary practice with the oracle of Simeon and the praise of Anna. From the Holy Family's journey to a foreign land, through the dreams of Joseph and the return of the family to Nazareth in Galilee, this couple chosen by God, see and experience their lives within the context of God's fulfillment of his promises.

This all began for Joseph when God awakened him to the truth about Mary's son. On the morning of the angel's visit, he began to grasp the God of his ancestors in an entirely new way. The Spirit, fully present in Mary, impacted the life of Joseph as it had impacted the infant John in the womb of his mother Elizabeth. Through Mary, the grace of God that is the Holy Spirit poured into Joseph's life, transforming his mind and heart according to the mind and heart of the child his wife carried.

In the days that followed the child's birth, right up to the time of Jesus's public ministry, Mary and Joseph spent their days simply doing whatever God required of them. This of course meant attending to all the regular demands of family life, like keeping house, providing for the family, and educating Jesus. They built a life for the child, mindful that every undertaking was for God. Through the Spirit, the bond of love in the life of their family, Mary and Joseph knew no lack in any spiritual gift as they awaited the revelation of Jesus Christ. From the moment the child took his first breath, Jesus was enough for them.

Through the gentle movement of God's Spirit—mysteriously yet concretely present in the Person of Jesus—Mary and Joseph show us how being faithful to God demands attentiveness to our vocations. The Holy Spirit guides them toward a fitting perception of what they have been asked to do. He teaches them how Jesus alone defines and therefore enriches every aspect of their lives. This child, destined for the fall and rise of many, is Life! Thus, whatever Jesus may need from them is their vocation. Whether it's cleaning or cooking, teaching or playing—every aspect of caring for and raising this child is an integral part of God's grand plan of redemption.

Through the dynamic engagement of the Spirit in their lives, Mary and Joseph willingly say yes each morning to all that is required of them, even to the unexpected—such as their flight to Egypt. They say yes to—and positively embrace—all the ways in which God will manifest his presence in the child they love and care for. Through their willing yes to God, they strengthen the bond of love that encompasses their lives through the same Spirit by whom Jesus—in his flesh—remains united with the Father.

The records of the evangelists provide no indication that Mary and Joseph learn in exact detail just how Jesus will save us from our sins. The little bit we know of the time between Christ's birth and the start of his public ministry presents the picture of a mother and father wholly engaged in the raising of God's Son. The Holy Spirit wasn't given to reassure them with intricate explanations in moments of confusion or to calm them with sudden insights about how trying times fit God's plan. Rather, the work of the Spirit is to assure those who love God that everything works for good through the grace of the Lord. Mary and Joseph will live these days in confidence, recognizing the presence of God in the child they are raising.

The Holy Spirit Accompanies Mary during Jesus's Public Ministry

The same confidence with which Mary and Joseph raised Jesus to manhood should characterize all those on whom the Spirit of God rests. This was certainly the case with John the Baptist. "Filled with the holy Spirit even from his mother's womb" (Luke 1:15), John knows the day will come when he will behold the Messiah and witness the Spirit descend upon him John is fully aware that he has been sent before the Christ—the Bridegroom—that he is only the best man. John could say about the unfolding ministry of Jesus, "This joy of mine has been made complete" (John 3:29).

Mary, like John, also knows something of the intensification of joy that comes with the increasing signs of God's promises being fulfilled. The words she sang when visiting her cousin Elizabeth already indicate how the Holy Spirit has touched her life with an enthusiasm and appreciation for the God who lifts up the lowly and fills the hungry with good things. Mary dramatically demonstrates this appreciation at the beginning of Jesus's public ministry, when she is with him and his disciples at a wedding in Cana.

On the third day, Mary notices something that could have disastrous implications for the couple. No doubt moved by the Holy Spirit, she takes it upon herself to present the situation to her Son: The wedding couple has no wine. Having seen the hand of God permeate her days with real signs of his presence, Mary is confident that God can do the same for this couple.

In this place where Jesus's disciples first begin to believe in him, Mary truly demonstrates what it means to hear the word of God and follow it. For Mary, this demands a selfless attentiveness to the needs of others and an unshakable resolve that Jesus can give men and women what they ultimately need: the love of God poured into their hearts like new wine. She heard from the angel Gabriel that her Son would be God's personal response to the emptiness of humanity, deprived as it is of God's life because of sin. Ever since the rejection of God's friendship, the human family has had no "wine." They've lived without the inebriating effects of God's life.

Mary listened well to the words of the angel: She knows that she enjoys God's favor; she knows that with God, nothing is impossible. She lives her life wholly intent on the needs of others, just as God has throughout history been attentive to mankind's need for him.

Through the gift of the Holy Spirit, the love of God operated in Mary from the moment of her conception. Her utter trust in her son prompts her words to the servers, "Do whatever he tells you" (John 2:5). Mary doesn't tell Jesus what to do or challenge his perplexing reply, "My hour has not yet come" (John 2:4). Her heart is in sync with the movement of the Spirit, and so she is convinced that the couple will receive what they need. The confidence with which Mary embraces her vocation and faithfully adheres to the Father's plan lies at the heart of her desire to share Jesus with others.

The Holy Spirit overshadows Mary, so that she might embrace and joyfully carry out all the requirements and responsibilities of her vocation. Singleness of purpose allows her the freedom to share Jesus with others. In the words of St. Paul, she hands on what she herself has received from the Lord. She has no need to possess Jesus as her own. One thing alone is required: to faithfully undertake all the demands of being his mother. This fidelity in turn provides the necessary setting in which Jesus can reveal himself as God's Son. Through the Holy Spirit, Mary already experiences the freedom for which Christ has come to set us free. She knows that every work for God is significant.

This freedom in the Spirit compels Mary to accompany Jesus throughout his public ministry, as mother and as disciple. The two vocations are one and the same for Mary, just as the Holy Spirit is inseparably God's gift and his love. Mary travels with her son, with absolute trust that God will complete the good work that began when she said yes to the angel Gabriel. Mary detects the Father acting through, with, and in her Son—however the Father chooses!

Many of Jesus's disciples will question his ability to feed the multitudes, calm the wind and seas, and give his flesh as life for the world. Mary never falters! Even at the end, she stands at the foot of the cross (John 19:25), continuing to breathe with the same Spirit that allows her Son to cry out, "My God, my God, why have you forsaken me?" (Matthew 27:46).

And when at last Mary holds the beaten, bruised, lifeless body of her crucified son—the rejected and humiliated Christ—still within her heart are the words formed long ago by the Holy Spirit. In the midst of her unspeakable pain and unimaginable suffering, she sings to herself over and over again, with a strength that comes from above and a consolation that only the Spirit gives:

> The Mighty One has done great things for me,
>   and holy is his name. (Luke 1:49)

The Holy Spirit and Mary after the Death of Jesus

The apostle John recounts for us the last act of Jesus's public ministry: entrusting his mother to John's care. Only when John has taken her into his home is Jesus aware that his work is finished (John 19:28). Jesus breathes his last knowing that Mary will have a home, with someone to love, care for, and protect her. The horrors of the cross cannot dull the love the eternal Son of the Father bears for the woman through whom he took flesh and was born into the world.

The words Jesus speaks from the cross issue from the mysterious bond of love that has existed between him and his mother even before she conceived him in her womb. Jesus, in the last moments of his physical life, reveals that the predestination of Mary as mother of the savior is a vocation that encompasses more than merely giving him birth and raising him to manhood. God has willed that this woman full of grace bear the firstborn among many brethren. Her spiritual motherhood extends to all of us who are redeemed by her Son.

The Spirit, who has touched Mary's life from the moment of her conception, has prepared her for this ministry of spiritual motherhood. All the gifts that God imparted to Mary, he gave with the entire community of believers in mind. Nothing from the

Father is given for an individual alone. The gifts from above are given so that, from Christ our head, all men and women might experience the grace we have received in him.

Therefore, it seems clear to me that Mary is the first gift or grace given to the Church, well before the morning of Christ's resurrection. Through her, Jesus is already fulfilling his promise not to leave the disciples alone. Although this assurance to the apostles refers to the Holy Spirit, who better to prepare them for the good things to come than the woman whose entire being is interwoven with the Spirit's? Mary's physical presence necessarily incarnates a spiritual strength to help them pass through the first agonizing hours of Jesus's death. The insights she carries in the depths of her virginal heart, doubt-free, will help them understand that all is not lost, that God's promises are being fulfilled—even against everything they feel.

Mary is the first person to show us how our relationship with Christ prevents even the most horrifying events and unbearable sufferings from defining or defeating us. Who better to remind the followers of the Christ that they are lacking in no spiritual gift while together they wait for God's plan to unfold?

Mary's role with the company of Jesus's followers changes with the announcement that Jesus has been raised from the dead. She recedes from the scriptural picture as Jesus's disciples struggle to comprehend what resurrection from the dead means. We can imagine her going off to a quiet place to ponder this extraordinary event in her heart. She knows that her Son is the best one to prepare his disciples for everything that is yet to come. Jesus has much to teach them before he ascends to his Father, and Mary will remain with them once he has. In the days following the resurrection, I'm sure that the moments Mary and Jesus shared together were for themselves alone.

The apostles and other followers of Jesus will need Mary's presence once Jesus ascends to the Father. Who better to teach them patience than the mother Christ has seemingly left behind? This time of waiting with the Church crystallizes Mary's universal maternity. She knows well how to pray in the holy Spirit and to keep herself in the love of God. She knows what the disciples can expect when the Spirit of truth comes upon them (John 14:17), what they will experience when they realize that Jesus is in his Father and they are in Jesus and Jesus is in them. Who better to explain this mysterious communion to them than the woman whose very being has been inextricably part of the very life of God?

Mary's position in the fledgling community demonstrates the necessity and the beauty of the Church's many ministries. Although she received God's Son in her womb and raised him up to fulfill the Father's plan, she remains perpetually God's handmaiden. She, who is in fact the mother of the Lord, never lords it over anyone in the community of Christ's body. I consider this humility most beautifully expressed every time she receives her Son sacramentally from the apostles. The woman who could make the greatest claim on God makes no claim whatsoever. Like every member of Christ's body, Mary steps forward, saying with greater intensity than any of us could muster, "Lord, I am not worthy that you should enter under my roof."

Through the gift of the Holy Spirit, Mary has learned that waiting is an experience of redemption. She waited for her miraculous baby to be born, for her Son to begin his public ministry, for the sign that it was completed; and now she waits to be reunited with him forever at God's right hand. In this way, she makes her election and call firm, showing the followers of her son that their entry into the eternal kingdom of our Lord and savior Jesus Christ will be provided. Mary is the ultimate custodian of the memory of Christ, and she shares this memory with the Church as it awaits the revelation of the children of God (Romans 8:19). Her life, wedded to God's through, with, and in the Holy Spirit, makes her always a true citizen of heaven. Thus she continues to teach the Church to await the Savior, the Lord Jesus Christ.

CHAPTER FOUR

The Holy Spirit in the Life of the Church

When the time for Pentecost was fulfilled, they were all in one place together. And suddenly there came from the sky a noise like a strong driving wind, and it filled the entire house in which they were. Then there appeared to them tongues as of fire, which parted and came to rest on each one of them. And they were all filled with the holy Spirit and began to speak in different tongues, as the Spirit enabled them to proclaim. (Acts 2:1–4)

*T*he familiar scene recounted in this passage from Acts often overshadows the earlier sending of the Holy Spirit, immediately after the death and resurrection of Jesus. As noted earlier, the first expression of what I call the event of the Holy Spirit happened on Easter Sunday. Jesus appeared to the apostles, who were hiding in fear behind locked doors. Breathing on them, he said, "Receive the holy Spirit. Whose sins you forgive are forgiven them, and whose sins you retain are retained" (John 20:22–23).

Although this moment is separated in time from the reception of the Holy Spirit at Pentecost, the two accounts do not contradict each other. Jesus did truly impart the Spirit to his apostles gathered in the Upper Room, and the Holy Spirit was sent by the Father to the Church gathered together—around the apostles—at Pentecost. There is no scriptural discrepancy on the part of the evangelists. To grasp fully the role of the Holy Spirit in the life of the Church, it is necessary to place these distinct moments side by side.

The Church underscores this point in her teaching on the anointing of Christ. While the Holy Spirit is with the Son from the moment of his conception in Mary's womb, the Church also affirms the significance of the dynamic revelation of the Spirit at the time of Jesus's baptism by John in the Jordan River.

> The Spirit whom Jesus possessed in fullness from his conception comes to "rest on him." Jesus will be the source of the Spirit for all mankind. At his baptism "the heavens were opened"—the heavens that Adam's sin had closed—and the waters were sanctified by the descent of Jesus and the Spirit, a prelude to the new creation. (CCC 536; see John 1:32–33; Isaiah 11:2; Matthew 3:16)

The Holy Spirit "Convokes" the Body of Christ

With this in mind, we can say that through the first outpouring of the Spirit, the Church, in a sense, becomes incarnate. Jesus breathes his life into the Church, represented by the apostles and other followers gathered together in the Upper Room. In this outpouring of the Spirit, they are constituted as the body of Christ, which is clearly built upon the firm foundation of the apostles. Through the second outpouring of the Spirit at Pentecost, each believer is filled with the gifts necessary to adhere to Christ and journey on toward the fullness of God's kingdom.

Through these distinct but complementary passages, we learn that the Holy Spirit is sent from above to convoke, or gather together, the followers of Christ. In doing so, the Spirit unites them not only with Christ, their head, but also with each other. Like the Father and Son who are eternally wedded to one another in the Holy Trinity, each member of Christ's body—through the power of the Holy Spirit—is wedded to the others.

This makes the Church something far greater than a voluntary association of those who choose to follow Christ. We actually become members of Christ's body. Through the living, vital bond of love between the Father and the Son—the Holy Spirit—we are united in a way that transcends whether one is Jew or Greek, male or female, slave or free. The Holy Spirit has come into the world to call together those from every tribe and tongue, people and nation, to make of them a kingdom for God (Revelation 5:9). The lives of all members penetrate those of the others. In the Holy Spirit, we share with our brothers and sisters, right now, a communion of life like that of the Father and Son, a communion of love that will be fully known when we share eternal life at the end of time.

The Spirit gives life to those so gathered. He functions as the soul of Christ's body. Through the manifestation of the Spirit, given to each member individually and to the apostles and their successors, the Church extends in space and time the anointing of Jesus. Just as his words and deeds—and every characteristic of his life—make present and appreciable in history the invisible reality of God, so does the Church, constituted by the Spirit, make the presence of the invisible Christ apparent in the world. When the community of Christ's body lives the new life received from the Holy Spirit, Christ's mission continues. When the Church truly lives according to the Spirit who gives her life, she experiences deep union with the Lord and is therefore able to make faith in him possible.

This faith, to which all men and women are called in Christ, was the reason for Jesus's being sent and anointed by the Father. Jesus came with the redemptive power of love to save us from our sins and gather us into the family of God, in order to unite all things in himself. While his death on the cross is the definitive atonement for human sinfulness, it is also the means by which this new family will be born in the world. In accordance with the wisdom and goodness of the Father, Jesus suffers and dies so that we might be raised up to share in his own divine life. He promises the Holy Spirit to his disciples, knowing that only with this Advocate can the company of his followers truly become children of God, according to the Father's plan.

First and foremost then, the Church is described as the sacrament of our inner union with God. The outpouring of the Holy Spirit makes the Church both the goal of God's infinite plan for humanity and also the means for achieving it. The Holy Spirit establishes the Church as an inextricable part of the mystery of salvation. By her nature, the Church is the primary instrument by which Christ manifests and realizes the mystery of God's love for the human family.

Through the outpouring of the Holy Spirit on Easter Sunday and Pentecost, the company of Jesus's followers becomes the visible plan of God's love for humanity. In them, the family of God is gradually formed and takes shape as they preach the Good News—the coming of the reign of God. Through the strength, courage, and insight they receive as fruits of the Spirit, these once timid followers set about extending the kingdom of heaven on earth so that it might be brought to completion at the end of time.

While awaiting the fullness of God's kingdom, the Church remains a part of history, growing and progressing through the efforts of her members. The same Spirit who makes the Church a visible reality also constitutes her as a spiritual reality that bears divine life. Through faith we are able to see how the Church always transcends history. She is a communion of men and women with God in the love that never fails.

The Church is therefore structured according to the purpose of charity (love). The pattern of her structure was received from Christ. The years the twelve spent with Jesus, their experiences with him personally and with his ministry, built them up and prepared them for the ordering of the community that would take form after Jesus's death, resurrection, and ascension into glory. This small flock became the true family of Jesus, as he taught them a new way of seeing themselves and of being in the world.

Just as Jesus intentionally called the twelve to follow him, he also selected Peter to serve as their head. This choice was confirmed by Jesus after he rose from the dead. It continued after he returned to the Father. It was Peter who stood up in the midst of the brothers and encouraged them to select someone to replace Judas as a witness to Jesus's resurrection (Acts 1:15–26).

Together the apostles and other disciples (about one hundred and twenty) shared in Christ's mission and his power. Through the gift of the Holy Spirit, they were able to do the works of Christ—and even greater ones besides. Their aim was to live the new commandment of love expressed by Jesus. "No one has greater love than this, to lay down one's life for one's friends" (John 15:13).

On the night before he died, Jesus, anticipating his sacrifice on the cross for our salvation, instituted the Eucharist as a perpetual sign of his loving commitment. Through the power of the Holy Spirit, the bread and wine offered that night were substantially changed to communicate his very life. At that first Eucharist, the Church anticipated the mystery of the new covenant in Christ's blood, a mystery "fulfilled" the following day when blood and water flowed from the pierced side of Jesus. St. Ambrose beautifully expressed it: "As Eve was formed from the sleeping Adam's side, so the Church was born from the pierced heart of Christ hanging dead on the cross" (CCC 766, quoting St. Ambrose, *Commentary on the Gospel of Luke*, 2, 85–89: PL 15, 1666–1668).

Through his death and resurrection, Jesus accomplishes the work of the Father. It is time then for the company of his followers to be his witnesses to the ends of the earth. The Advocate whom Jesus has promised them is sent on the Day of Pentecost, to sanctify them and push them out into the world. With the dynamic reception of the Spirit, those who have been hiding in the Upper Room begin to openly preach the Gospel in the same city where Jesus was put to death. No longer afraid of the consequences of being his followers, they boldly share their faith in Christ to the inhabitants of Jerusalem as well as the pilgrims gathered there on the occasion of the feast. The love they have for Jesus is transformed by the sanctifying power of the Spirit into a love that "bears all things, believes all things, hopes all things, endures all things" (1 Corinthians 13:7).

In the power of the Holy Spirit, the disciples now are capable of fulfilling the mission Jesus entrusted to them. Receiving from the Spirit the very gifts of Christ, this small company of disciples becomes the seed and the beginning of God's kingdom. Jesus's prediction is now fulfilled: "When the Advocate comes whom I will send you from the Father, the Spirit of truth that proceeds from the Father, he will testify to me. And you also testify, because you have been with me from the beginning" (John 15:26–27). Through the power of the Holy Spirit, this convocation is suddenly full of strength. The apostles are able to say, "Jesus is Lord" (1 Corinthians 12:3), and cry out in the depths of their hearts, "Abba! Father" (Galatians 4:6).

The Holy Spirit Inspires Sacred Scripture

The apostles experienced firsthand the fact that God wills everyone to be saved and to come to knowledge of the truth. Emboldened by the Holy Spirit, they begin on Pentecost to proclaim Christ as the fulfillment of Israel's hope. In what is arguably Peter's first homily, he speaks enthusiastically to the Jews—and all those staying in Jerusalem—about the way Jesus fulfills everything promised beforehand by the prophets. Peter is absolutely insistent that the man Jesus, who was crucified by lawless men, has been released from death to be made both Lord and Messiah. Through the very Person of Jesus and through the Holy Spirit, God worked "mighty deeds, wonders, and signs" so that all those who repent and are baptized might be filled with joy in God's presence. Peter's proclamation that "Jesus is Lord" is the Good News that God longs all men to hear. Peter used many other words in his testimony that day, all of them directed at explaining Jesus to them, for Jesus is the Gospel.

The apostles learned a great deal from everything Jesus said and did and from the way he lived his life. Now, under the guidance of the Holy Spirit, they are able to recall the details of his life within a broader perspective. The Spirit enhances the perspective Jesus gave them about God, themselves, and others. This forms the basis of their teaching from the early days, as the community devotes itself to the breaking of bread and to prayer.

The apostles work many signs and wonders, always adhering to the Lord's command to make his salvation known to the ends of the earth. Through their words and deeds, the example of their lives, and the institutions they establish, the apostles incarnate God's love. Their lives become events in which others truly encounter Christ, in every circumstance, joy and struggle. The Gospel is handed on as they share this inspired activity with those who are joining their company.

In time, the rapid growth of the Church prompts some of the men associated with the apostles to put down in writing the message of salvation. Through the inspiration of the Holy Spirit, these individuals firmly, faithfully and without error record what they hear proclaimed. They set down in writing that truth which God inscribed in the sacred Scriptures.

The belief that God could speak through human words wasn't foreign to the apostles. In times past and in partial and various ways, God had spoken to their ancestors through the prophets. Now, through the inspiration of the Holy Spirit, the apostles grasp how God has spoken one Word, his Son, "Whom he made heir of all things and through whom he created the universe,

> who is the refulgence of his glory,
>   the very imprint of his being,
> and who sustains all things by his mighty word. (Hebrews 1:2–3)

"Christ, the Son of God made man, is the Father's one, perfect, and unsurpassable Word" (CCC 65).

The apostles are attentive to the Holy Spirit, who instructs them in everything concerning Christ. They know that, in order for the living voice of the Gospel to dwell in all its richness in the hearts of believers, they need other men to assist them. They select certain ones to participate in their ministry and to succeed them in it.

To these bishops the apostles entrust the same authority to preach and instruct the faithful as they received from Christ. Through the bishops and the inspired books of Scripture, the apostolic preaching has been preserved in a continuous line of succession. The full and living Gospel is preserved until the end of time.

As described in the first chapter, this personal transmission of the faith has its roots in the Old Testament. The Spirit of God, given to Jacob and Saul and Elisha so they could carry out God's plan for his people, has been given to the bishops for the same purpose. The Church refers to this person-by-person transmission of the faith as Tradition. While it is distinct from Sacred Scripture, it is nevertheless bound to it. Both by this personal means of handing on what has been received from God and by the Scriptures, the Church perpetuates and transmits to every generation the doctrine, life, and worship that define who she is and everything she believes. This transmission of the faith is the singular grace of the Holy Spirit.

The same Spirit by which the apostolic preaching is passed on from generation to generation was at work in all the authors of Sacred Scripture. Throughout the history of man, God has inspired human beings to compose all that he wanted to share with us about the truth of who he is. However, the individuals chosen by God did not take dictation. Rather, God's Spirit acted in them and through them, using their personal talents and capabilities to commit to text whatever God wanted and nothing more.

This unique relationship between the living Tradition and the written Word continues to distinguish the Christian faith from other religions. Christianity is a religion of encounter. Through and in the Holy Spirit, we have access to the incarnate and living Word of God. We have been gathered together by the Spirit to manifest the eternal Word of the living God in everything we say and do. The Holy Spirit instructs us in the Scriptures, making them as living and vital as Jesus, the man whom they reveal.

The Scriptures should therefore be read within the life and faith of the Church. They are handed down from generation to generation as the living memorial of God's Word. This precious treasure issues from the very heart of the Church, wherein lies the bond of love between Father and Son. It would be impossible in one lifetime to grasp the height and depth and breadth of all that the Scriptures contain, because God is always far greater than anything we could say about him. The mystery of his love is unbounded.

Years ago, at the opening Mass of a parish mission, the deacon of the Word leaned toward me and said, "This is going to be difficult for you; everything that can be said about tonight's Gospel passage has been said." While the deacon certainly meant well, the sentiment he expressed is simply untrue. As the soul of the Church and the source of inspiration, the Holy Spirit guarantees that there will always be something more to be gleaned because the Word of God can never be exhausted.

The Church desires all the faithful to find in the Word of God "strength for their faith, food for the soul, and a pure and lasting font of spiritual life" (CCC 131, quoting *Dei Verbum*, 21). The Church encourages all the faithful to grow in the surpassing knowledge of Jesus Christ by meditating on the divine Scriptures under the guidance of the Holy Spirit. As the great Scripture commentator St. Jerome said, "Ignorance of the Scriptures is ignorance of Christ" (CCC 133, quoting St. Jerome, *Commentary on Isaiah*, book 17 prol.: PL 24, 17b; see Philippians 3:8).

The Holy Spirit, Source of Life in the Church

As we previously discussed, God sent the apostles to preach the Good News so that all the nations of the world would know Christ. Through their words and way of life, these men continued to manifest the Church to the world just as on the Day of Pentecost.

Through the outpouring of the Holy Spirit, the convocation of those who believed initiated a new age in which Christ would both express and make present his work of salvation, particularly through the Church's life of prayer, the sacramental liturgy.

Belief in the Lord Jesus necessarily entails active engagement with the members of his body. This convocation, brought together by the outpouring of the Holy Spirit, is organized according to a definite purpose. The Spirit is sent by the Father and the Son to establish the Church as the primary means by which the fruits of Jesus's passion, death, and resurrection are dispensed in the world. The ordering of the body of Christ according to the seven sacraments he instituted during his public ministry (the sacramental economy) is the principal means by which God, through the power of the Holy Spirit, blesses us in Christ with every spiritual blessing. There can be no true life in Christ without full participation in the life of his body, the Church.

More than just a gathering of Jesus's followers, the Church has its origin in the Father's eternal desire to bless us with his life. This hope of the Father has come to pass through the words of his Son and the gift of his life. In Christ we are destined for adoption according to the favor of God's will (Ephesians 1:5). Now we exist for his glory being able to adore the Father and offer him our lives in thanksgiving for his grace, which has been poured out on us in Christ Jesus his Son.

It seems to me, then, that an essential component of the New Evangelization must be the presentation of the Church as the fundamental source of the Father's blessing. Every aspect of the Church is solely for this purpose. Established by the Holy Spirit, the Church rightly exists as the culmination of everything God has been up to for men and women since the first moment of creation. The covenant with Noah, the election of Abraham, the birth of Isaac, the Passover from Egypt, the entrance into the Promised Land, the kingship of David, the building of the Temple as a sign of God's presence, even the exile to foreign lands and the return of a small but faithful remnant—all were leading up to the new age of the Church.

This shows us that the Church's liturgy is something far greater than merely the way that Catholics pray on Sundays. Through word and sacrament, the assembly of the faithful acknowledges and adores the Father as the source of all blessings in a unique and unheard-of way—in the way of the Son. Through the liturgy of the Church, the Father's blessing is fully revealed and communicated. Praying as one body with Christ our head, the Father in turn pours into our hearts the Gift of love that unites us to one another and to Christ: the Holy Spirit. The Church, through this wedding of lives, is the beloved bride of Christ who calls to her Lord and through him offers worship to the eternal Father.

While the Church is truly a community of believers, it is only one to the extent that her members regularly participate in the sacramental economy. The sacramental liturgy is the fitting context for the response of faith and love that is owed to the Father for the indescribable gift he has bestowed on us in Christ (2 Corinthians 9:15). In the Holy Spirit, we are able to offer the Father adoration, praise, and thanksgiving, not only as ourselves but as the Son. In him we beg the Father to send the Holy Spirit upon our offerings, ourselves, and the world until the end of time.

Jesus had to return and take his seat at the right hand of the Father. His ministry on earth could not be completed without the sending of the Holy Spirit. Through this gift of Love enlivening the Church, Christ continues to communicate his grace in a perceptible way in the words and actions of the sacraments. These efficacious signs are inextricably bound to Christ's own paschal mystery, for which he prepared his followers throughout his life on earth.

The hour he expressed the Father's love through his self-offering does not pass away; Jesus's paschal mystery does not remain in the past. Everything Jesus did and all that he suffered for us and our salvation touches us in the present. Jesus died, was buried, and rose from the dead once and for all. Through the power of the Holy Spirit, we participate in his cross and resurrection.

The proclamation to every human creature that the Son of God, by his death and resurrection, frees us from the power of sin and death and brings us into the kingdom of his Father must surely entail access to this saving mystery. The Risen Christ enabled this by pouring out the Holy Spirit on the apostles and the Church. Through this Gift of Love, Jesus bestowed upon his body the anointing he received from the Father, so that they, too, might sanctify people with the divine life.

Through the outpouring of the Holy Spirit, the apostles become sacramental signs of Christ, efficacious instruments of his saving mysteries. Through no merit of their own, they are ordained to invoke the Holy Spirit in order to dispense the richness of the Father's blessing, which was made visible to them in Jesus his Son. Through the same Holy Spirit, they impart this power of sanctifying to their successors, thereby guaranteeing in time and history that the structure of the Church remain fundamentally ordered to the sacramental economy until the end of time.

Christ remains truly present in his Church and continues his work of salvation through every member of his body. Through the sacramental liturgy, he associates every action with himself, for "where two or three are gathered together in my name, there am I in the midst of them" (Matthew 18:20). The earthly liturgy therefore offers a foretaste of the heavenly liturgy, where Christ is seated at the right hand of God.

In the liturgy the Holy Spirit instructs the assembly in the faith and prepares them to encounter their Lord. Through the Scriptures, the Spirit recalls the words and deeds of Jesus; and through the sacraments, he offers the life of the Risen Christ so that all might live. In all things, the Holy Spirit attempts to arouse a genuine response of faith, in order that the liturgy might truly be a cooperative work, a communion that truly unites the Church to the life and mission of Christ.

Thus the new covenant established in Christ's blood is expressed by means of liturgy, especially in the celebration of the Eucharist and the sacraments. Every liturgical action effects an encounter with Christ through the communion effected by the Holy Spirit. This communion is not an ideal or an abstraction. The people— just as they are—gather together. This communion demands not simply acknowledging one another as members of Christ's body but really loving one another—not as we want others to be or as they should be but as they are, with all their weaknesses, sins, limitations, and, too, their gifts.

The liturgical assembly should be a place of challenge and trust, confirmation, and growth. This is how the unity of the Spirit is manifested and how the children of God are transformed into the one body of Christ. This recognition of each person the Holy Spirit has assembled looks beyond all racial, cultural, social, and, indeed, all human attractions.

This type of communion, which is the work of the Holy Spirit, requires that the people who gather are prepared to encounter the Lord. When the Spirit of God hovered over the waters of creation, he was already preparing the entire universe and even the human heart for the blessings of the Father. Working through signs and wonders and the words of the prophets, the grace of the Spirit awakened faith, converted hearts, and disposed men and women to obey the Father's will. These preconditions for the reception of the graces to be conferred by Christ endure in the new age of the Church. They open the faithful to the fruits of new life now conferred by the celebration of the liturgy of the Church.

According to the mysterious plan of God, the work of carrying on the salvation won for us by Christ is intended to be a collaboration of the Holy Spirit and the Church. While the Church enacts the liturgy, it is the Holy Spirit who gives it life, for the liturgy is not orchestrated according to the memory of those who gather to adore and thank God but through the Spirit. The Holy Spirit serves as the living memory of the Church, giving spiritual insights into the Word of God to those who read or hear it, so that they can live what they celebrate. He uses the words, actions, and symbols of the celebration to bring everyone gathered together into a living relationship with Christ.

The liturgical assembly should first and foremost be a communion of faith, because the liturgy of the Church not only recalls the events that saved us but makes them present. The Church doesn't repeat these events. In each celebration, the Holy Spirit makes uniquely present the mystery of Christ's saving love. The priest begs the Father to send the Holy Spirit, that the bread and wine may become the Body and Blood of Christ and that the faithful, by receiving them, may become a living offering to God. The most intimate cooperation of the Holy Spirit and the Church is achieved in the Mass.

Every time the Holy Spirit is invoked, the Father sends him, in obedience to the desire of his Son. Their collaboration seeks to bring us into greater communion with Christ as members of his body. The Spirit, the communion of love between the Father and the Son, abides indefectibly in the Church and makes her the great sacrament of divine communion. Thus, as branches on the vine, we may bear fruit that lasts unto eternal life.

The fruits that the Spirit bears in the life of the Church were announced and prepared in the words and actions of Jesus during his hidden life and public ministry. By the power of the Holy Spirit, who guides her into all truth, the Church discerned over time that among her liturgical celebrations are seven sacraments that, in the strict sense of the term, were instituted by Christ. Through these seven sacraments, Jesus meets the members of his body at significant moments of their lives, pouring into them the healing and strengthening grace of his love. The Holy Spirit assures the faithful that God hears their cries and has not abandoned them.

The sacraments are an integral part of the liturgy of the Church and the primary means by which the mission of the Holy Spirit is experienced. They sanctify the members of the Church, build up the body of Christ, and give fitting worship to God. When the Church celebrates the sacramental liturgy—especially the Eucharist—she confesses the faith received from the apostles. The Church prays what she believes and believes as she prays, celebrating the mystery of the Lord until he comes, when God will be all in all.

From the foundation of the Church at Pentecost, the sacramental liturgy has drawn the Church toward her goal by the Spirit's groaning, "Come, Lord Jesus!" (Revelation 22:20). The liturgy is a share in Jesus's desire: "I have earnestly desired to eat this Passover with you…until it is fulfilled in the kingdom of God" (Luke 22:15). In the sacraments of Christ, the Church already receives the guarantee of her inheritance, sharing even now in everlasting life, as we await the appearance of the glory of God and of our savior Jesus Christ.

The Holy Spirit Enables the Church's Mission

Christ's Passover was fulfilled on the Day of Pentecost. The Holy Spirit, promised by Jesus, was abundantly poured out upon those gathered in the Upper Room. In this unmistakable moment of overwhelming grace, God revealed himself as Trinity. The Spirit, once envisioned as an attribute of God, was then experienced as a divine Person uniquely bound in relationship with both the Father and the Son.

On that glorious day, the kingdom Jesus announced after his

baptism in the Jordan was open to anyone who believed in him. By humbly turning away from sin and accepting in faith that Jesus is Lord, three thousand began to share in the communion of love that is the Holy Trinity. The Church became the living embodiment of the kingdom by the unleashing of the Spirit. Now she awaits that kingdom's final consummation, when Christ will return in glory.

The Church's goal is to bring to completion the mission of Christ and the Holy Spirit: the eternal plan of the Father that all women and men share his life. While Christ was sent to reveal the Father's plan, it is only through, with, and in the Holy Spirit that we can be drawn into the life of the Father through the flesh of his Son. On the Day of Pentecost, the Spirit manifested to the Church gathered in prayer the real, vital, enduring presence of the Lord, whom they had witnessed ascending to the Father. The nascent Church was able to understand the meaning of his death and resurrection. And when they gathered to celebrate the Eucharist, the Holy Spirit made the mystery of Christ present to them in the breaking of the bread and the sharing of the one cup. Through the Eucharistic species, they experienced in a tangible way the reconciliation Christ won for them, and they understood their responsibility to go and bear fruit that would last unto eternal life.

The dramatic event of Pentecost reveals the true nature of the Church. Far from being an addition to the joint mission of Jesus and the Spirit, the Church is a sacrament of what the Father sends her members to accomplish. In her whole being and in all her members, the Church is sent to announce, bear witness, make present, and spread the mystery of the communion of the Holy

Trinity. Christ, who is head of the body constituted by the Church, pours out on his members the same Spirit with which he has been anointed. This vibrant expression of divine love nourishes, heals, and organizes Christ's body. He gives the functions necessary to bestow God's own life, bear witness to the sacrifice of the cross, forgive sins, and intercede on behalf of the whole world.

Through his holy and sanctifying Spirit, Christ communicates himself to the members of his body. In the sacraments, every member of the community is built into a living edifice of God in the Spirit and bears fruit through the new life received from Christ. This fruit is primarily manifested through concrete acts of the charity of Christ. It is rooted in the acceptance of God's goodness and mercy and fueled by the sure and certain hope for what has yet to be revealed.

Only in the Church does the Spirit of the living God truly flourish. Only in the Church can man truly experience the utterly gratuitous and mysterious plan of the Father, that all people might share in his divine life.

Those whom the Spirit gathered in the Upper Room on the Day of Pentecost were sent to spread the Good News. Each one received specific gifts of the Spirit, so that together they might carry on the ministry of Christ and make disciples of all nations. The Church is by nature *missionary* (that is, "sent"). Her soul and sanctifying presence is the Spirit, who proceeds eternally from the Father and the Son to bring life to the world.

The Holy Spirit has endowed the Church with the very gifts of Jesus, her founder, so that she can faithfully observe his precepts of charity, humility, and self-denial as she goes about proclaiming and establishing among all peoples the kingdom of God. The Holy Spirit not only bestows the necessary hierarchic gifts and spiritual charisms but also directs the Church's use of them. Thus the Church is able to fulfill her mission.

As the "soul" of the body of Christ, the Holy Spirit is the agent of every vital and truly saving action in each member. Each such action, in turn, builds up the whole. This begins with the sacrament of baptism, by which one dies and rises with Christ. The Holy Spirit is continually at work in the other sacraments, by which each member can find healing and experience new growth in the Lord.

The presence of the Holy Spirit is wonderfully displayed in the virtues of her members, the saints of the Church, both living and dead. We also see the Spirit's presence displayed in the many special charisms that embolden the faithful to undertake various tasks and offices for the renewal of the Church. Every charism, whether extraordinary or simple, is a grace the Holy Spirit imparts in order to directly or indirectly build up the Church, promote the good of others, and care for the needs of the world. No charism is given solely to benefit an individual member of Christ's body.

Thus each authentic charism of the Spirit should be accepted with humility and gratitude by the person who receives it, as well as by all members of the Church. The charisms are rich graces for the apostolic vitality and holiness of the entire community of Christ's body, provided they are genuine gifts of the Holy Spirit and are used in full conformity with the Spirit's promptings.

Of course, as with all things concerning the life of the Church, charity is the true measure of charisms. The discernment of charisms is always necessary; no charism is exempt from the oversight of the shepherds of the Church, whose responsibility it is to test everything and retain what is good, so that all the diverse and complementary charisms work together for the common good. Just as the Holy Spirit could never act against the Father and the Son, no member can claim that a charism—allegedly received from the Holy Spirit—compels him or her to act against the Church.

Years ago I had a student explain to me that the Holy Spirit had given him permission to do something that opposed the moral teachings of the Church. I had to explain—patiently and with charity—that while a spirit may have encouraged the behavior, it certainly wasn't the Holy Spirit!

That being said, throughout the history of the Church, special gifts and charismatic leaders have regularly and unpredictably emerged for the education of the whole of Christ's body. These gifts and leaders can only function effectively if they allow themselves to be nourished by the institutional and stable elements of the Church, such as Sacred Scripture and the sacraments. At the same time, the institutional offices, which are an integral part of Christ's body, should never forget that they can be enlivened by authentic charisms that are intrinsically related to their ministries. For example, a man to be ordained must demonstrate that the Lord is calling him to service in the community and that the Holy Spirit has bestowed on him the gifts necessary for fulfilling this ministry of service.

All public representatives of the Church are only credible to the extent that their lives conform to the Lord, that their lives literally incarnate Christ. This is especially incumbent upon souls whose priestly identity is most clearly expressed in the Eucharist. Priests must live out the mystery they are privileged to celebrate, or they shouldn't celebrate it.

The letters of St. Paul provide us with an outstanding record of the Holy Spirit pouring out gifts on the newly born Church. Yet even in recounting this overwhelming outpouring of graces, St. Paul makes it clear that every gift claimed as coming from the Spirit must be rooted in and ordered toward the Person of Christ. In the case of the Christian community at Corinth, which seemed to have a superabundance of gifts, the members appear to have forgotten the mystery of the cross and resurrection. Thus Paul warned against the exaltation of the gifts without reference to Christ and his paschal mystery. He considered this the pathway to self-destruction. "Nobody speaking by the spirit of God says, 'Jesus be accursed'" because the work of the Spirit consists precisely in leading believers to confess, "Jesus is Lord" (1 Corinthians 12:3).

Like many aspects of the Church, her nature is not a question of either-or but of both-and. The outpouring of the Holy Spirit on Easter Sunday affirms the institutional dimension of the Church, grounded in the Person of Christ. When considering the outpouring of the Holy Spirit at the dynamic event of Pentecost, we see the charismatic dimension of the Church grounded in the Holy Spirit. Yet there is only one Church, one Spirit, one Lord, who is over all and through all and in all. The Pentecost event occurs only because Christ has already pledged to never abandon the Church.

Christ has objectively guaranteed the final victory. This

objectivity, rooted in the Person of Christ, pertains to the sacraments and their efficacy, the inerrancy of sacred Scripture, and the infallibility of the teaching office. Sadly, throughout history these truths have been rejected by individuals and groups who claimed to know better the mind and purposes of the Holy Spirit. This objective truth remains a stumbling block to some believers.

This is not to deny the very real tension between the institutional elements of the Church and the charismatic. This tension, however, is rooted in the Person and mission of the Holy Spirit, who "scrutinizes everything, even the depths of God" (1 Corinthians 2:10). In the inner life of the Holy Trinity, the Spirit is entirely receptive. He "makes known to us Christ" and "makes us hear the Father's word, but we do not hear the Spirit himself" (CCC 687).

The Holy Spirit is always the Spirit of the Father and the Son and eternally bound to them in love. This determinative quality of the Holy Spirit is the ultimate foundation of everything institutional in the Church. The Father and the Son determine all her "stable" elements. However, this is only one aspect of the Spirit's life within the Trinity. As the ecstasy of God, the Holy Spirit is also the superabundant fruitfulness of the Father and the Son's love. Thus the Holy Spirit also represents the freedom of God—the infinite and unimaginable creativity of the divine activity.

It appears that St. Paul had this in mind when he told the community at Corinth that the Holy Spirit brings freedom. The Holy Spirit personifies the love between the Father and the Son and thus is the determining form of divine freedom. He personifies the freedom of the Father and Son to give themselves to one another. Freedom is the very nature of the Spirit's existence.

By itself, therefore, the institutional Church will never be able to adequately express the Trinitarian purposes of God for the world. The Spirit will always transcend the institutional, because it is the Spirit's mission to be creative, to interpret the meaning of Christ in the world in ever unpredictable ways. The Church is not meant to live in mindless imitation or in a petrified recreation of the past. The Spirit is always orienting the Church toward the future, when all will be one in Christ.

The greatest sign of how the Spirit manifests this freedom in the life of the Church is the saints. In every age God grants us new expressions of holiness—men and women whose unique missions represent what the Spirit is up to in the Church and saying to the world. Their presence is a living sign of the Church's vitality. Guided as the Church is by the Spirit, the institution can never suppress the God-given charisms of the saints.

As a student of Church history, it's quite clear to me that the mission of the Church will inevitably be carried out in this tension between the institutional and the charismatic. But this is not a contradiction. Because this tension is rooted in the very life of the Trinity, it will always be creative for the Church. The Spirit as the bond of love is our access to participation in divine life. Thus a contradiction is impossible.

In the life of the Trinity, the Spirit is ever bound to the Son (the institutional). At the same time, as ecstasy, he is always directed beyond (the charismatic). The mission of the Holy Spirit is to move the Church ever more toward her destiny. He does this in liberating ways that are yet always determined by the Person of Christ.

CHAPTER FIVE

The Holy Spirit in the Life of the Believer

Yet we do speak wisdom to those who are mature, but not a wisdom of this age, nor of the rulers of this age who are passing away. Rather, we speak God's wisdom, mysterious, hidden, which God predetermined before the ages for our glory, and which none of the rulers of this age knew; for if they had known it, they would not have crucified the Lord of glory. But as it is written:

> "What eye has not seen, and ear has not heard,
>   and what has not entered the human heart,
>   what God has prepared for those who love him,"

this God has revealed to us through the Spirit.

For the Spirit scrutinizes everything, even the depths of God. Among human beings, who knows what pertains to a person except the spirit of the person that is within? Similarly, no one knows what pertains to God except the Spirit of God. We have not received the spirit of the world but the Spirit that is from God, so that we may understand the things freely given us by God. (1 Corinthians 2:6–12)

*J*esus began his public ministry announcing, "The kingdom of God is at hand," and calling people to repentance (Mark 1:15). Through his ministry of reconciliation, Jesus offered more than lofty ideas about a spectacular and unimaginable future. For those with ears to hear, he offered participation in the life of God. The Father, whom Jesus revealed by his words, deeds, and way of life, longed to draw all people together in himself through his Son. Jesus's call to repentance was an invitation to turn the whole of one's life to the Father, who loves us despite our being wounded by sin. Jesus preached a God of love who longs to pour into our hearts the same love that constitutes his own life.

The teachings of Jesus were often difficult to accept, so many people refused to believe in him or the works he did. To those who accepted the truth that Jesus had the words of eternal life (John 6:68), he promised to send an Advocate, the Spirit of Truth" who would remind them of all things and lead them to all truth. The Father's love is comprehensive: He wants all men to come to the knowledge of the truth—a knowledge that reaches within. Jesus didn't come simply to reveal God; he came to bring God into our lives, so that we could know God even as we know the Son.

The Holy Spirit Fulfills God's Promises

The conversion that Jesus preached is the first work the Holy Spirit effects in the life of the believer. This action of grace moves the heart away from that which diminishes or even destroys one's humanity and toward God, the giver of life. The Holy Spirit convicts the believer regarding sin in order that the person might better appreciate the salvation God offers in the death and resurrection of Christ.

With this conviction of sin comes the recognition of forgiveness. The offer of divine life is an expression of mercy. "For God did not send the Son to condemn the world, but that the world might be saved through him" (John 3:17). The gift of life offered by the Holy Spirit corresponds to the deepest desire of the human heart, the longing to be whole.

Once we allow the love of God into our hearts, we are able to live no longer for ourselves but for him, with heartfelt charity and in genuine solidarity with other men and women. The ability to love as God has loved us is a sign that the Holy Trinity dwells within and expresses our new life in Christ (1 John 4:11–12). By this power of the Spirit, God's children are grafted onto the True Vine, in order to bear the fruits of "love, joy, peace, patience, kindness, goodness, generosity, faithfulness, gentleness, self-control" (Galatians 5:22–23). The better able we are to renounce ourselves, the better able we are to follow the Spirit. When our identity is fixed firmly on the solid foundation of Christ, we begin to experience our humanity in all its richness.

When the Spirit awakens in our hearts the desire to turn away from sin, he also opens our minds to Christ. And in Christ we can penetrate the mystery of the Father and his love. We are able to see in Christ the image of the invisible God, and we become aware of our own exalted vocation to be sons and daughters of the Father.

The Spirit is willingly sent by the Father and the Son in order to unite us with Christ and allow us to see ourselves as the Father knows us in the eternity of his mind. We can become God's children—now. We are adopted as sons and daughters of God. The Spirit imparts the graces we need in order to follow the example of Christ, to act rightly and do good deeds.

This new life in Christ, which God longs to give us, comes to us through the sacrament of baptism, which was part of the Church's life even before her birth at Pentecost. And on the Day of Pentecost, all those moved to repentance through Peter's proclamation of the Gospel were encouraged to be baptized in the name of Jesus Christ for the forgiveness of sins and to receive the Holy Spirit. Later the apostle Paul, for whom the Holy Spirit occupied a central place, preached the importance of baptism as the means of being united with Christ:

> Are you unaware that we who were baptized into Christ Jesus were baptized into his death? We were indeed buried with him through baptism into death, so that, just as Christ was raised from the dead by the glory of the Father, we too might live in newness of life. (Romans 6:3–4)

The Holy Spirit hovers over the water of baptism, in which we are purified, justified, and sanctified.

By the power of the Holy Spirit, baptism cleanses us from sin and makes us alive for God in Christ Jesus. With the righteousness of God (that is, his life) dwelling within our bodies—as in a temple not made by human hands we are clothed with Christ and become members of his body, heirs in hope for all the good things of God. Indeed, we are so associated with the exalted Christ that St. Paul alternately describes our life in the Spirit as life in Christ, contrasting this with life according to the flesh.

St. Paul promises that if we put on Christ, our mortal bodies will one day be raised in the likeness of Christ's resurrected body.

Through the Spirit, the Father offers us a life that precludes every imaginable separation from his own. The bold claim of Christianity is this: Through the outpouring of the Holy Spirit, our lives can become one with the life of the Triune God!

To establish this, the Holy Spirit heals the wounds of sin, transforming us from within by the renewal of our minds and hearts. By this justification, we are called to be saints and to live as children of the light, glorifying God in our bodies, conforming our thoughts, words, and actions to the attitude that is ours in Christ. By the power of the Holy Spirit, we are incorporated into Christ in order to be "imitators of God, as beloved children, and live in love" (Ephesians 5:1–2).

This walk in love has discernible traits. In uniting us with Christ, the Spirit bestows the virtues necessary to be children of the light. God is the source of "whatever is true, whatever is honorable, whatever is just, whatever is pure, whatever is lovely, whatever is gracious" (Philippians 4:8). The firm attitudes and stable dispositions by which we govern our actions and order our passions all reflect our having been created in the image and likeness of God.

Although we are wounded by sin, our natural disposition is toward that which is good and true and beautiful. Being made for God, our hearts retain a desire for fulfillment in him, even if this cannot be named. Through the grace of the Holy Spirit, whatever natural virtues we possess become rightly ordered to our supernatural destiny.

Of course, this requires our openness to everything God wants for us. The fulfillment of God's promises cannot be realized until we surrender our attitudes, dispositions, habits, and passions—indeed, anything that has previously determined our way of life—to our newfound knowledge of Christ. This surrender comes through the movement, guidance, and inspiration of the Holy Spirit. "Everyone should always ask for this grace of light and strength, frequent the sacraments, cooperate with the Holy Spirit, and follow his calls to love what is good and shun evil" (CCC 1811).

In order, then, that we might live fully our new life in God received through the sacrament of baptism, the Holy Spirit infuses in us the capacity to live here and now as God's children, even as we await the hope of eternal life. These new theological virtues are wholly compatible with all human virtues and are definitive signs of the presence of God's Spirit acting in concert with our human faculties. It cannot be stressed enough that this sending of the Holy Spirit is a gift far surpassing mere knowledge of what Jesus accomplished by his death and resurrection. The Holy Spirit comes as a gratuitous act on the part of each member of the Trinity, so that we can become one with God and live this in our redeemed humanity.

God's promises are thus fulfilled in us to the extent that our lives express the virtues that only emanate from us through the work of the Holy Spirit.

Faith

The first of these virtues pertains to our belief in God, not only in the written works that have been preserved and handed on but also in everything the Church proposes about the truth of God and how we come to know him. Through the subtle but enticing work of the Spirit, we desire to know ever more fully the God whose love has been revealed in Jesus his Son. Thus we commit our lives to knowing God's will and accepting it.

The virtue of faith must never be reduced to an intellectual enterprise or a simple mastery of religious information. The virtue of faith is always and only expressed in the words and deeds that characterize our confession of Christ in all aspects of our lives. The virtue of faith is ultimately a principle of identity, the very measure of how we understand and manifest the truth of who we are.

Faith, since it is oriented toward Christ, is that rock on which Jesus told his disciples they must build their lives. The Holy Spirit reawakens in us the truth that we have been created in the image and likeness of God. Therefore, no physical, social, political, ethnic, or even sexual criterion can be the basis on which a person builds an identity. All past and present-day attempts to build on such criteria are direct results of the wound of original sin.

No matter how much we may empathize with the current trend to define oneself and create one's own identity, this tendency is ultimately destructive. It deprives a person of his or her God-given dignity, beauty, and truth. For those who have been united with Christ and have allowed the Holy Spirit to move freely in their lives, Christ encompasses the truth of their being and is the foundation of their identity. "I live, no longer I, but Christ lives in me; insofar as I now live in the flesh, I live by faith in the Son of God who has loved me and given himself up for me" (Galatians 2:20).

Hope

As the Spirit works within our spirits to show us Christ and teach us the mysteries of God, our perception of what is ultimately fulfilling changes. To summarize the words of Scripture, hope is born in our hearts, and this hope is not determined by personal expectations about the world or about ourselves. The virtue of hope, instilled by the Holy Spirit, provides us with an entirely new horizon. Placing our trust in the promises of Christ, we set our sights on those things that will never pass away, especially the love of God. St. Paul reminds the young bishop Titus why Jesus came into the world: He came to pour out the Spirit upon us, "so that we might be justified by his grace and become heirs in hope of eternal life" (Titus 3:6–7).

Like the virtue of faith, which awakens our innate sense that there is something greater than us, the virtue of hope corresponds with our innate desire for happiness. The overwhelming goodness of the Spirit prompts us to see that our plans and achievements, our prior goals and expectations, cannot compare with life forever within the kingdom. This kingdom life alone is what will truly satisfy us. Through the gentle guidance of the Spirit, we come to recognize that the things we once thought would fulfill our desires to be whole, complete, and at peace—no matter how good they may be in themselves—cannot possibly satisfy those desires. The Spirit leads us to understand happiness not as a deeply felt emotion, a sentiment, or a manmade achievement but as union with God in his kingdom.

The virtue of hope, which is instilled by the Spirit through our incorporation into Christ, is the only sure safeguard against letting the arduous conditions and circumstances of life determine our well-being. The hope that is ours in Christ, a hope rooted in faith, keeps us ever centered on the love that is our destiny. While we may experience real pain and terrible frustrations, hope preserves us from debilitating discouragement and the bitterness and resentment that can result from it. This is why St. Paul told the Christian community in Rome, "Rejoice in hope, endure in affliction, persevere in prayer" (Romans 12:12). If his words were not true, then they would be exceedingly cruel.

The hope that the Holy Spirit instills in the hearts of those who believe is rooted in the ministry of Christ. Jesus promised that all those who love and obey God will enjoy the beatitude described in the Sermon the Mount. Jesus revealed a Father who is ever present to his children and always willing to give them whatever they need (Luke 11:9–13). Jesus proclaimed the kingdom of God in hopeful terms. He promised to go before his disciples in order to prepare a place for us (Hebrews 6:19–20).

Love

The Holy Spirit wishes to inculcate in the heart of each believer the very principle of the divine identity: love. This is the charity Jesus defines as the new commandment. The love that is the source of his being is also the source of ours.

While the old law prescribed love of God and neighbor, Christ's willingness to be crucified has broadened that command. On the night before he died, Jesus made it clear that love can only be expressed in a willingness to sacrifice—to love to the end. Christ has asked us to possess his very love, even for our enemies.

(Indeed, we were enemies of God before Jesus was born into the world to reconcile us.)

Jesus didn't simply make demands; he showed us the full extent of what love means. In case his suffering and death aren't example enough, while hanging on the cross he forgave a prisoner crucified next to him. Jesus extended to this guilty man the most incredulous promise: "*Today* you will be with me in Paradise" (Luke 23:43, emphasis mine). And for those crucifying him, he prayed, "Father, forgive them, they know not what they do" (Luke 23:34).

Even many who do not know Christ and many who reject the notion of a God agree that love is what makes us fully alive and most fully ourselves. Love might make a person blind or be the cause of reckless choices and questionable alliances, but every human being longs to be loved and appreciated, to be special and be wanted. The virtue of charity most corresponds with our having been created in the image and likeness of the God who is love. As St. Paul so beautifully puts it, "If I...do not have love, I am nothing" (1 Corinthians 13:2).

The virtue of charity is the purpose of human existence. "Love is itself the fulfillment of all our works. There is the goal; that is why we run: we run toward it, and once we reach it, in it we shall find rest" (*CCC* 1829, quoting St. Augustine, *Commentary on the Gospel of John,* 10, 4; PL 35, 2057).

Every human virtue is ordered toward charity, and so too are faith and hope. "Love...binds everything together in perfect harmony" (Colossians 3:14, *RSV*), so that the peace of Christ can reign in the human heart. This peace is the tangible experience of Christ in the lives of those who believe.

Jesus comes to tell us that we are God's friends—not slaves, not hirelings, but sons and daughters whom he has come to search for and carry back to the Father. The fulfillment of God's promises is the virtue of charity, by which we are able to love the God who first loved us. The only condition for receiving this grace of the Spirit is our ability to let God love us.

The Holy Spirit Provides Us with the Gifts to Follow Christ
God loves the world and his desire is that all men and women share his life. This is the central tenet of Christianity. Jesus didn't come merely to save us from the fires of hell; he came to give us eternal life.

Through the sacrament of baptism, we receive God's life, and the Trinity immediately dwells in us, placing an indelible mark on our souls. The Father, the Son, and the Holy Spirit all act uniquely for this purpose. As I've mentioned before, the divinization of the human person is the fulfillment of God's plan for us. We are to be "filled with all the fullness of God" (Ephesians 3:19).

The specific way in which the life of God is united with our own is through the Holy Spirit. We can say that Christ lives in us because the Spirit that binds him in love with the Father has been poured into our hearts. The Church refers to the indwelling of the Holy Spirit in the life of the faithful as an uncreated grace, because the Holy Spirit is one in being with the Father and the Son. Together the Father and the Son send the Spirit, to incorporate the believer into the life of Christ, in order that the individual can then have access to the Father. Our ability to relate to each member of the Holy Trinity, individually and personally, is the Father's plan.

At the Last Supper, Jesus went to great lengths to underscore this teaching. He told his disciples: "Whoever loves me will keep my word, and my Father will love him, and we will come to him and make our dwelling with him" (John 14:23). Later St. Paul would stress the same idea, reminding the faithful that they have become temples of the Holy Spirit. "Do you not know that your body is a temple of the holy Spirit within you, whom you have from God?" (1 Corinthians 6:19). We should remind ourselves every day of the truth that the Trinity dwells in each of our lives. Imagine if every Christian began the day mindful of who he or she has become in Christ.

Through the outpouring of the Holy Spirit, we are both justified and sanctified. This uncreated grace empowers us to collaborate in the ministry of Christ. Thus the life of Jesus may be made visible in our mortal flesh. The Holy Spirit comes not for us alone but for the salvation of others. Through the Spirit mingling with our spirits, we learn the hidden ways of God and receive the gifts necessary to build his kingdom here and now. United with Christ, we can draw others to share his life as members of Christ's body.

In order to sustain our life in Christ, the Holy Spirit has entrusted the Church with the stable and necessary means to nourish and strengthen her members. The Scriptures, the sacraments, and everything handed on through Tradition communicate graces that are proper to them. The Holy Spirit works through all these essential elements on behalf of the community. Each member of Christ's body should experience the effects of this working.

The Church celebrates the sacraments of initiation in a way that reflects the two different moments of the outpouring of the Spirit recorded in the Scriptures. Like the Church hidden behind locked doors on Easter Sunday, before baptism we are locked behind the door of original sin. Jesus breathes on us in baptism, and we receive the Holy Spirit in order to become members of his body, the Church.

At confirmation, just like those gathered in the Upper Room at Pentecost, we receive a special outpouring of the Holy Spirit that deepens what began in baptism. The Spirit does for us now what he did for those disciples: He gives each of us special gifts that unite us more firmly to Christ. Through these gifts we can, in word and deed and every dimension of our lives, truly be witnesses of Christ and defenders of the faith. This sacrament of confirmation is essential to our life as members of Christ and of the Church.

The special gifts of the Holy Spirit received through confirmation are elements of justification that can continually renew the presence of the Spirit in our lives. In the writings of St. Paul and the Acts of the Apostles, we have vivid descriptions of the presence and activity of the Holy Spirit in the lives of the just. Thus, being confirmed in our union with Christ entails a willingness to participate always with his Spirit. We bear the Spirit in the concrete conditions and circumstances of everyday life.

Just as the prophet Isaiah foretold that the Spirit of the Lord would come to rest on the Messiah, so in the sacrament of confirmation the Spirit of the Lord comes to rest on us. He takes the same form:

> a spirit of wisdom and of understanding,
> a spirit of counsel and of strength,
> a spirit of knowledge and of fear of the Lord. (Isaiah 11:2)

These gifts enable the believer to adhere more easily to Christ, even in obscure and complicated situations. They enable the faithful to come to right decisions in spite of confusing clashes of reason.

We were created for God. Even after the original sin of our first parents, we continue to possess a natural openness to God. The gifts of the Holy Spirit are useful adjustments of this openness that is intrinsic to human nature. They also keep in check the forces of self-assertiveness, selfishness, and concupiscence that constantly wage war with the inspirations of grace.

God is eternally active, and the Holy Spirit is constantly creating anew the qualifications for the acceptance of the divine in us. Each individual believer needs these gifts in life's ever-changing situations. The Spirit works different effects according to the contours and demands of those situations. His goal is to help each person hold fast to his or her relationship with God.

The individual, even though justified by the Spirit, can sever or harm the many bonds that tie him or her to Christ's body. We cannot neglect the gifts of the Spirit, which are necessary for our own well-being and that of the Church. How many times do we long for the right words to say and yet forget to ask for the gift of counsel? How often do we not feel like praying or feel as if we are simply going through the motions in prayer? Do we beg for the gift of piety? As we prepare ourselves for Mass on Sundays, are we whispering over and over again, "Piety, piety, piety"?

What do we do in situations that test our patience and challenge our love of neighbor? Do we beg the Spirit for strength and understanding? If we truly knew the Gift of God, we would indeed be demanding it all the time!

The community of Christ's body is essential for the salvation of the individual believer, and the gifts of the Spirit further the life and growth of the community in its understanding and its love of Christ. In St. Paul's First Letter to the Corinthians, the gifts of the Spirit are given an "ecclesial" interpretation. They are seen as manifestations of the one body of Christ that help build it up. These unpredictable but nonetheless indispensable gifts are meant for special tasks in special situations of Church life.

> Now you are Christ's body, and individually parts of it. Some people God has designated in the church to be, first, apostles; second, prophets; third, teachers; then, mighty deeds; then gifts of healing, assistance, administration, and varieties of tongues.... Strive eagerly for the greatest spiritual gifts. (1 Corinthians 12:27–28, 31)

The Spirit's gifts that touch the intellect are understanding, wisdom, knowledge, and counsel. They all primarily pertain to the domain of faith and its realization in the world. In no way are they substitutes for human study. They provide insights into the mystery of salvation, always pointing the faithful toward the horizon of God.

The gifts of the will are piety, fortitude, and fear of the Lord. They have nothing to do with superstition or magic but instead enable the faithful to love and adore the Father and to join with other women and men in building up Christian fellowship. With the help of these gifts, we are able to be steadfast in hardships, trials, and dangers without becoming fearful or falling into despair. These gifts help us recognize in our historical situations the demands of God's will.

St. Paul seems to have presupposed that a Christian community is necessarily a charismatic community. Among the many created graces or charisms, he mentions speaking in tongues, teaching, healing, and prophecy. In the first centuries of Christianity, it seems the Christian faithful expected such gifts. It makes me wonder what would happen today if once again we lived with this same expectation.

With the passage of time, the Church, understandably, became more institutionalized. Thus charisms were often appropriated by the prescribed offices of the community. Although waves of charismatic activity have been a recurring phenomenon in the history of the Church, the Catholic community, at least in recent centuries, has tended to be very suspicious of charisms, even seeing charismatic people as a threat to the institutional stability of the Church.

Yet the record provided by the New Testament makes it clear that the sacraments and official ministries of the Church were not the only means by which the Holy Spirit sanctified and enriched the Church with virtue. The Spirit distributes special graces among the faithful of every rank, "to each person as he wishes" (1 Corinthians 12:11). By these gifts, he makes people able and willing to undertake various tasks or services beneficial for the renewal and building of the Church. According to St. Paul, "To each individual the manifestation of the Spirit is given for some benefit" (1 Corinthians 12:7). These charisms, whether they are infrequent or widely dispersed, should be received with gratitude, for they are suitable and extremely useful for the Church.

Our life in God can only develop and flourish by the power of the Holy Spirit. The Spirit works to preserve the roots of immortality onto which we have been grafted through our baptism into Christ. The new life we receive depends upon the graces the Spirit provides to each of us individually and to the Church as a whole. Like St. Paul, we should constantly speak to God on behalf of all members of Christ's body, bowing before the Father that he might grant them to be strengthened through his Spirit.

This inner, spiritual man matures and grows strong through the Spirit. The human spirit which knows what pertains to a human person, meets the Holy Spirit who understands everything, even the depths of God. The Holy Spirit truly opens himself to us, enabling our human spirits to open in their turn before the saving and sanctifying self-opening of God. This is an experience of the reciprocal openness that pertains between the Father and the Son. In the mutual openness of the Holy Spirit and us, we will experience "what eye has not seen, and ear has not heard" (1 Corinthians 2:9).

The Holy Spirit Is Our Hope for Everlasting Life

The Church continues to proclaim the mystery of Pentecost and to celebrate it in the sacrament of confirmation. The Holy Spirit has established the Church as his dwelling place, the permanent witness to Christ's victory over death, and the instrument by which Christ's presence continues to be manifest in the world. God who raised Christ from the dead will give life to our mortal bodies also, through his Spirit that dwells in us. Resurrection is life, and this life, proclaimed by the Church, is experienced in the Person of the Holy Spirit. Together with Christ, the Spirit longs that everyone might have life, even those who are now dead because of sin.

Through the gifts or created graces imparted by the Holy Spirit, the baptized are brought into the supernatural reality of the divine life. The Christian becomes a dwelling place of the Holy Spirit, a living temple of God. In communion with the Holy Trinity, human life is expanded to transcend natural life. Baptism enables us to live in God. In God's Spirit, our minds and hearts are raised to the things that are above. The more open we are to the work that God is up to in our lives, the more set our minds become on the actions—graces, charisms, gifts—of the Spirit.

This integral communion of God's life with our own shines light upon how we understand our humanity. The Spirit frees us from the common categories by which human beings typically try to figure themselves out. The only operative standard of judgment becomes the one that was established when God breathed life into the male and female—namely, our being made in his image and likeness. The spiritual and the incorruptible transcend all material concerns.

This innate truth of our humanity is dramatically rediscovered in the light the Spirit shines upon the Person of Christ. In this light we see the Son's relationship with the Father as the only true way to be in relationship with God. The self-sacrificing love that lies at the heart of this relationship with the Father is the key to our own unique and irreplaceable humanity. What we learn from Christ's life and the teachings of the Church emerges as the truth of our own being. Through the Holy Spirit acting in concert with our own spirit, we are truly able to give ourselves to Jesus Christ as he gave himself to us.

No one understands this more than Mary, Jesus's mother. She knows the depths of this interior awakening to the truth of humanity. She wants the entirety of our lives to be assumed into the life of the Trinity. Thus the Spirit who overshadowed Mary urges us toward her maternal care.

As together with the Holy Spirit we travel along this new path of interior maturity, God draws ever closer to us, and through us he is able to more effectively permeate the world with his presence. This intensive and often frightening action of grace isn't something we can orchestrate or control. It comes through genuine surrender to the Holy Trinity.

The transformation Christ came to effect happens first and foremost within our own minds and hearts. The graces given by the Holy Spirit, uniquely fashioned for the needs of each member of Christ's body, enhance the development of God's kingdom until such time as he may be all in all. The eternal power of the Gift-Love that is the Holy Spirit opens the world to God and God to the world through the lives of the members of Christ's body.

Under the inebriating influence of the Paraclete, we discover the freedom of the divinization of our lives, both as individuals and as members of Christ's body. The various strangleholds that mainly grow out of materialistic ways of thinking and acting wither. The degenerative social factors that so easily and subtly penetrate the inner recesses of our hearts and souls give way to the freedom that comes in being a child of God.

We desperately need the Holy Spirit to shine light on our union with Christ and to cast out all the pressures exerted by the social structures that intrinsically oppose the truth of human dignity. Today there are many social factors that do not foster the development and expansion of the human spirit. More than ever before, we need the Holy Spirit to keep vigil within us and protect us from the "prince of this world."

Everyone born to new life through the waters of baptism is a witness to human dignity. By our interior cooperation with the gifts the Spirit creates in us, we can be agents of the renewal of the world. Charity compels us to work with others and to use everything that is good, true, beautiful, and just—in every area of thought and human activity—to advance what St. John Paul II called a "civilization of love."

Christ is at work within the men and women who possess the life of the Holy Trinity. By the power of the Holy Spirit, he becomes Lord of our lives and stirs within our hearts his own eternal desire that all women and men experience the loving communion of God. His desire is that every culture and society reflects lasting justice and real peace until the consummation of all things at his return.

The Christian hope for everlasting life, however, is more than just an expectation of the future glory of the last day. Everlasting life—being raised with Christ—begins at baptism: "You were buried with him in baptism, in which you were also raised with him through faith in the power of God, who raised him from the dead" (Colossians 2:12). This new life we share with Christ is strengthened, encouraged, and directed by the graces the Spirit

gives us in confirmation, so that here and now we can participate in the death and resurrection of Christ. We should therefore
constantly strive to seek what is above, where Christ is seated at
the right hand of God.

Yet how well we know that this risen life we share with Christ
is hidden with him in God. We may sit with him in the heavenly places, but life here can be filled with injustice, suffering, and
pain. It can be difficult to understand how the arduous conditions
of life and death can have positive meaning.

St. Paul considered death to be a gain. But when we witness
the death of others—especially the innocent, the young, and our
own loved ones—and when we face our own death, we encounter
true challenges to our belief that we are already living the new life
Christ promises. We know we have died with him in baptism, and
yet we also know that we must physically die.

The resurrection affirms the goodness of human bodily life. In
Jesus's real human body, we participate in the salvation he won
for us. This is why, against all reason, the apostolic preaching was
insistent about the cross, about Christ crucified. The justification
and salvation affected by the Spirit are not some mystical or senti-
mental experience. Rather, through our incorporation into Christ,
we share with him—in real, visceral, substantial ways—the salvation he won for us.

We have been totally united with the Trinity, and this necessarily includes our bodily lives. It isn't just our spirits that have
been united with the Holy Trinity; it is both our souls and our
bodies. God's love is unimaginably generous: He holds nothing
back, not even the life of his Son.

Through our physical death, we complete the dying and rising that began in baptism, and the Father summons us to his bosom, just as he summoned his Son. Christian death can be the ultimate expression of obedience and love for the Father.

Only by the grace of the Holy Spirit is it possible to live this dying and rising in Christ that is a gift of baptism. The Spirit helps us understand the meaning of Jesus's words to Martha on the occasion of the death of her brother Lazarus: "I am the resurrection and the life" (John 11:25). Through the grace of the Spirit, with which the humanity of Jesus was anointed, Martha was able to accept the fact that Jesus was the Christ and that God would give him whatever he asked (see John 11:22).

In order to remain steadfast in the faith of being raised with Christ on the last day, it is imperative that our lives are immersed in the life of the community of his body. Here the Spirit has provided everything we need to remain ensconced in that everlasting life that is even now ours in Christ. Among all the graces the Spirit has given, Christ himself has left us the Eucharist as "the source and summit" of our lives as Christians (*Lumen Gentium*, 11). Each time we remember the death of the Lord until he comes, we share sacramentally in his "dying and rising" and are thus able to bear them in our own lives.

Through Christ's real gift of himself in the Eucharist, we experience everlasting life as the truth of our being here and now, even as it is a foretaste of all the good things to come. In the sacrament of the memorial of Christ's dying and rising to new life, we are united ever more intimately with the Holy Trinity. The Spirit convicts us of the truth that Jesus will raise our mortal bodies and make them like his own in glory.

The Holy Spirit, the Source of Our Prayer

The dramatic event of Pentecost happened within the context of prayer. The members of the Church were all gathered together in one place, awaiting the fulfillment of Christ's promises. We know from Scripture that they chose to await this Spirit of the Father and the Son by devoting themselves to the teaching of the apostles, prayer, and the breaking of the bread.

The gift of the Spirit that the apostles received on Easter Sunday was already at work within this convocation of Christ's body, to orient them toward Christ. They were mindful of everything they had witnessed and learned during their time with Jesus, both before and after his death and resurrection. When at last the fullness of the Spirit came upon them, they realized how the Holy Spirit forms and shapes communication with God.

Since the earliest days of the Church, there have been two common descriptions of prayer: speaking to God and raising the soul to God. Each tries to capture this great religious act that is a natural and fundamental human activity. Before we consider the transformation of prayer that occurred through the sending of the Holy Spirit, it is important to consider prayer from the perspective of God's creation of man and woman.

Prayer begins through our recognition of ourselves as creatures, finite and yet aware of something greater. It is an impulse that takes us outside of ourselves, inspired by the expectation of some deeper meaning or the longing for an infinite existence. Prayer doesn't issue from a sense of resignation about our condition but rather from a sense of hope: There must be something more. Through the act of prayer, a person attempts to reach beyond the boundaries of space and time and touch something transcendent, some ultimate Other who is responsible for everything that exists.

Prayer expresses an all-pervasive longing for happiness, not in terms of emotional satisfaction but in terms of personal fulfill-ment. The impulse that grounds the act of prayer is an uncondi-tional and sensitive openness to that which transcends all the ins and outs of everyday life. Prayer addresses the basic questions of human existence.

The Church has traditionally defined prayer as the ascent to God, as "pouring out [the] soul before the Lord" (1 Samuel 1:15, RSV), longing for God "as the deer longs for streams of water" (Psalm 42:1), and taking refuge in God. Within the ascent to God, man discovers the reality of his own transcendent being. Thus prayer becomes a commitment to the truth of his essence as well as a search for the mystery of his existence. Humility, reverence, and receptivity form the responsive stance to the One who we sense is the answer to the longings within our hearts.

The Church has always regarded prayer as a grace, a gift of the Creator. God fashioned us in such a way that our entire being could be open to him. And yet, prayer is always a free act on our part. God has created us to hear his call and has given us the ability to respond, but listening and responding must be human actions of the will.

This is perhaps most wonderfully observed in the meeting between Mary and the angel Gabriel. Here the call of God and human freedom perfectly meet each other, and the union of the two becomes the life incarnate in Mary's womb, a life that will both illuminate and permanently transform the human act of prayer.

Mary brings to her encounter with the angel an experience of prayer that was formed by the history of her people. The Scriptures of the Old Testament present the faithfulness of God as the context for all forms of prayer, with three distinct aspects. The first is the memory of the past: "He has delivered his people from the bondage of Egypt" .(Exodus 13:14). Recalling God's deeds was a common practice of the prophets, and it inspired the hymns and prayers of thanksgiving in the Wisdom literature.

The second aspect concerns the certainty of the present: "He will not...forget the covenant" (Deuteronomy 4:31). And the third has to do with the expectation of the great final deliverance: "See, your king shall come to you" (Zechariah 9:9).

The awareness of God's personal guidance was a significant component of the prayers of the Israelite community and the individual. In the last five centuries before the birth of Christ, this emphasis was stabilized in the Jewish liturgies, with which Mary would have been familiar. Through them she also embraced her people's sense of God's majesty. This was a God whose name could not even be uttered in prayer. This surely made Gabriel's words all the more troubling. Indeed, how could this be?

At the outset of his public ministry, Jesus demonstrated an entirely unheard-of approach to prayer, forgoing the religious legalism of the Pharisees. In the Sermon on the Mount, he expressed childlike confidence in his Father in heaven. He demonstrated his sense of security with respect to the Father, conversing with God as a child would speak to his father (Matthew 6:9–13).

In the Garden of Gethsemane and on the cross at Calvary, Jesus clearly showed the polarity of Christian prayer, a tension between the active and the passive. In his dialogue with the Father, Jesus begged that the cup of suffering might pass, but then he silently, reverently, and intentionally accepted it. Jesus could cry from the cross words that seem almost disrespectful, "My God, my God, why have you forsaken me?" but then hand himself into the Father's care.

This tension in Christian prayer reflects the tension we have discussed before with respect to the Holy Spirit. It is a creative tension that elevates our natural capacity for prayer to a supernatural level, so that we truly can address the majesty of God with the simplicity of a child. There is no doubt that Jesus's prayer reveals the perpetual unity of his will with that of the Father, a unity that is meant to be ours through the Spirit at work within us.

Jesus distinguished his prayer from that of others:

> When you pray, do not be like the hypocrites, who love to stand and pray in the synagogues and on street corners so that others may see them.... But when you pray, go to your inner room, close the door, and pray to your Father in secret. And your Father who sees in secret will repay you. In praying, do not babble like the pagans, who think that they will be heard because of their many words. Do not be like them. Your Father knows what you need before you ask him. (Matthew 6:5, 6–8)

Jesus taught the apostles to speak to the Father from one's heart.

The model of prayer that most influenced the way the early Christian community prayed is the Our Father. Jesus shared this prayer with his disciples for the simple reason that we can make it our own. The Church has incorporated the Our Father into her communal acts of prayer, and learned two things from this model Christ left us.

First, both individual and communal prayer should always express absolute confidence in the goodness and power of our heavenly Father. This became such a dominant aspect of the prayers of Christians in the early years of the Church that the certainty of being heard does not seem to have been a problem. Praying in the Spirit instilled within the community the assurance of God's providence, in whatever concrete historical terms it might be expressed. Prayer wasn't so much the act of telling God what should be done as it was an act of acknowledging and celebrating the fact that God was present, active, and doing exactly what needed to be done. Thus the apostles left the Jewish council after being flogged, "rejoicing that they had been found worthy to suffer dishonor for the sake of the name" (Acts 5:41).

The second thing the Church learned from Jesus through this prayer was the expectation of his return in glory. Nearly every prayer of the early Church focused on this. The confidence that God would respond to all the petitions of the community was rooted in the unshakable conviction that Christ would come again.

The Scriptures of the New Testament also show clearly that the interaction of the disciples with the risen Jesus and with the Holy Spirit were the standard of prayer. The followers of Jesus learned early in his public ministry how being close to him intensified their natural and religious desire to pray. The resurrection only deepened this experience. St Paul preserved this fact, by his constant use of the expression "through Christ."

St. Paul's own closeness to Jesus changed his understanding of prayer and the way he prayed. He knew that this ability to address God as one friend to another was only possible in the Holy Spirit, who is the bond uniting all the forms of prayer expressed by the early Church. Since it is the Holy Spirit who imparts to the community of Christ's body this new confidence in God, St. Paul exhorts his fellow Christians to "pray unceasingly" (1 Thessalonians 5:17).

The Holy Spirit, by focusing everything on the Person of the Lord Jesus, brings into wonderful harmony the three dimensions of Jewish prayer mentioned above. Thus the prayers of the Church look back to the historical action of God in the Person of Jesus, specifically his passion, death, and resurrection. The prayers of the Church also acknowledge the presence of the Lord in his body, the Church. This abiding, dynamic presence of Christ in the sacraments and in the members of his body inspires all of the Church's prayers. And of course, the Church still possesses the conviction of the first momentous days following Pentecost that the Lord will come again. This expectation of Christ's return surpasses the expectation of the Messiah preserved in the Old Testament Scriptures.

While the gifts of God cannot be weighed against each other, the transformation of prayer inaugurated by the Holy Spirit beautifully and perfectly manifests God's desire that we share his life. Through the living water welling up within our hearts, we are able to relate to each member of the Trinity in the uniqueness of their Persons. The life of Jesus is not merely imprinted upon our minds as incidents that God expects us to superimpose on everything we do. They are more than "interpretive keys" by which the confusions and complications of life are rightly understood.

The Spirit unites us to the life of Jesus. The surpassing generosity of God is that, through the Spirit, we can experience the Gospel events as if we were present for them. This does not happen only when the Church recounts them in her sacramental liturgy. Through his resurrection from the dead, Christ has united the whole of his human life to the eternity of Trinitarian communion. There, in the Spirit, we have access to the full life of Christ—as he sees fit—in order that we may become ever more fully the sons and daughters of his Father. The Father always knows just what we need, and he ministers this in terms of the actual historical life of his Son. This knowledge alone should compel every believer to be a person of prayer.

While we drink of the Spirit in and through the sacraments, we are also nourished by his presence every time our minds and hearts are lifted to heaven. The gentle, loving presence of the Spirit might be difficult for us to discern, but the fact that we have constant, regular, substantive recourse to Christ is a sure sign that we live in the Spirit. We can associate with any one of the many symbols or images of the Spirit to aid us in our prayers.

The Father has made it easy for us to pray. All we have to do is say, beg, or demand, "Come, Holy Spirit." Any desire we have for Jesus or the Father emanates from the Spirit united with our own.

The Church has always encouraged the faithful to find the means by which the heart becomes ever more secure in the knowledge of the Father's love. We are fortunate to have a rich treasury of devotions, prayers, and pious practices. The only prayer imposed by the Church is our communal acts of worship and thanksgiving, of penance and self-denial. Everything else is left up to each individual believer. There are as many paths of prayer as there are persons who pray. However we may construct our life of prayer, the same Spirit acts within us and within our neighbor, whose spiritual practices might be different from our own.

Prayer expresses our lived relationship with the Father, the Son, and the Holy Spirit. It transforms our lives according to the self-sacrificing love that defines the Son's life. A lived communion with God is always open to us, because we are united to Christ through baptism, and in confirmation the Holy Spirit has given us every gift needed for this communion.

Our lives in the Spirit (what many call "the spiritual life") are not means to an end but ends in themselves. Prayer isn't a way of garnering God's attention or safeguarding ourselves from his wrath. Prayer is the truest sign that we know—even against what we may feel—that we always have the Father's attention and the Son's support. Prayer is the true sign that we are living the divine life, the gift of love that has come to us from above.

*T*he twelve men Paul confirmed in Ephesus experienced the Holy Spirit as a mysterious bond of divine communion with Jesus, whom they had already accepted as their redeemer, and with the rapidly growing Church. Through this gift from above, they were able to appreciate the fact that Jesus's work depends upon everything the Spirit takes from Christ and imparts to his followers. On that day, through the openness of their hearts to God, the Holy Spirit entered their lives and the history of Ephesus.

The men in Ephesus were perhaps the first to learn that Pentecost is not meant to remain an historical moment of the Church but is to be an ever-present experience for all her members. These twelve men, an echo of the first apostles, came to know the Holy Spirit in the innermost sanctuaries of their souls. They were given the gifts necessary to help the Church in Ephesus continue to grow, as well as the gifts each one needed in order to live this new life in Christ. St. Paul called down the Holy Spirit to bring these men the peace and consolation the Father wants for all his children. To me, there's little doubt that, on the day they received the fullness of God's Spirit, the hearts within these men were on fire.

The great gift of love that St. Paul shares with this small convocation of Christ's followers is present whenever people are led to Christ. The Holy Spirit brings no new revelation; he recalls the things that Jesus already said and did. Any alleged novelty concerning the Person of Christ—anything incompatible with what has been preserved, taught, and handed on from the apostles—comes from an anti-spirit. The Holy Spirit is one with the Son, and he always moves us toward the Son. This movement is not a static look at the past but always a thrust toward the future, toward the consummation of all things in Christ. The Spirit moves us to the Son so that we might naturally move toward the Father.

What the Spirit says and brings about in Christ remains normative forever. Every true reform, every authentic scrap of human progress, must be consistent with the promised perfection of the heavenly Jerusalem. The Church will always put the memory of Christ to good use—not as nostalgia but as the proper means for each member of Christ's body to remain open to the free and powerful breathing of the Spirit.

We feel this "breath of God" when we welcome the presence of the Spirit rather than live according to the flesh or to the world: "For the desires of the flesh are against the Spirit, and the desires of the Spirit are against the flesh" (Galatians 5:17, RSV). Two great signs of the Spirit are freedom and love. For where the Spirit is, there is freedom And each person is given the gifts of the Spirit for the common good; the greatest of these gifts is love.

Thus, the greatest sign of the Spirit in our lives is the freedom to love, including the freedom to cast aside whatever squelches our capacity to love. The only obstacle to our ability to live the new commandment of love is in us. The Holy Spirit whispers this reality to our spirits; let us listen to that still, small voice.

Another great sign of the Spirit's presence within the community of Christ's body is the stamp of the cross and the glory it reveals. Our life in the Trinity is an immersion in the paschal mystery—the life, death, and resurrection of Christ. Although we may not literally bear the wounds of Christ in our bodies, we are united to him in the Spirit to bear this dying and rising within the context of our lives. The Holy Spirit glorified Jesus because of his total obedience to the Father on the cross and then raised him from the dead, so that Jesus could grant life to all who believe in him.

The Spirit continues to guide the Church and all her members, consistently encouraging the faithful to lose their lives in order to find them. The Spirit introduces us to Jesus in such intimacy that the power of infinite love mingles with our own response to him, no matter how timid that response might be. We breathe with the Spirit of God when we give life for love, offer consolation to those experiencing tribulation, extend forgiveness in the face of hatred and persecution, and remain confident and strong in times of persecution.

The Holy Spirit may be the most difficult Person of the Blessed Trinity to apprehend. But he is intensely present in the lives of believers. We have only to say, "Come, Holy Spirit!"